The "Spooky" Qubit
(From Quantum Mystery to Networked Application)

W. Houze, Ph.D.

Contents

Introduction

First, my target audience for this book is rather wide: from the intelligent lay reader who knows next to nothing about all things Quantum big or small, to the students and professionals who know a little more than the average person about the topic.

If you are not a physicist, a mathematician, or a computer scientist by formal training, all is not lost: the book is accessible to you on several levels. Chapters 10 and 11 do get a bit into the math weeds, but most of the book is, in my view, understandable if you have your wits about you and are willing to extend yourself to engage with subject matter that might at first seem to be off-putting or too esoteric to bother with in the first place.

I have an earned Ph.D. in literature and philosophy. I am not a computer scientist, a physicist, or a mathematician. But I am able to follow the logic and understand the basic concepts that are covered in the book from beginning to end. I find the content in Chapters 10 and 11 to be out of my depth of knowledge, but even so, challenging and interesting. It is an opportunity for entering a superposition state of being: I understand only if I do not look at it too closely!

I wrote over the last two years several books that focus on AI, and all of them were to one degree or another, designed to present to the reader my own dialog between one or more online AI engines (GPT, Claude, Copilot, Gemini). I created the organizational structure for the book, its outline. I created the questions that I posed to the various AI engines. I was responsible for the level of detail, the kinds of questions being asked, and steering the AI engines in various directions to get out of them the content I wanted to meet my goal and purpose in writing with them each book.

And for the record, not all of these books reflect my whole-hearted endorsement of AI in any of it many manifestations, purposes, utility value, accuracy by way of content out of AI, and the like.

In short, I find AI—which is not artificial at all, but one-off from human programmers, algorithm designers, LLM trainers, and dataset curators—to be a powerful tool that humans can apply in many situations and for good reason and to achieve positive outcomes.

But AI is old hat now. The mysterious and finicky horse named Quantum has bolted from its barn and is by now galloping at an increasing pace across the countryside—nay, around the globe itself.

Of late, therefore, I have been thinking not so much about the latest hype that seeks to propel OpenAI and other like-minded enterprises from rags to riches, but more and more about what the runaway horse named Quantum is all about.

This book, then, is focused on Quantum, and its stable-mate, Classical. As in Classical Computers and Quantum Computers, their co-dependencies, their foibles, their error rates, all the normal things that attend the emergence of a technology of the complexity—and quantum mechanical mystery—at the core of quantum computing.

So this book begins with the nature of the qubit and works its way from there through successive levels of detail about how a quantum state is created, how it can be marshalled via the classical computer to compute XYZ. And of course like any emergent technology, there are all kinds of risks, operational variables that are difficult to impossible to control, and the like.

All of these issues are addressed in the beginning and middle chapters in this book. I intended to build the bridge early on so the reader can cross the river of quantum mystery first in the shallow and more understandable depths of the subject; then, in the middle chapters, to continue along on the bridge, looking down in the currents of quantum unknowns that are moving just beneath the surface. Finally, when almost across the quantum river, the reader gets a chance to see in the water lapping the distant shore the images making up the concluding scene of luminaries.

The book also addresses what I thought was my own novel concept: a master quantum computer model that can be used in a controlled distributive manner via a classical computer front-end to task satellite classical-quantum computer systems running in a linked and isolated framework. Like the runaway horse Quantum, these satellite setups could be anywhere on Earth—and even in Space.

But I was not the first to come up with this concept. Many others beat me to it, and they are given prominence in their sections of the book.

The book ends for the reader who takes the risk and walks across the bridge from the first chapter to the last with my personal favorite part: an imaginary scene featuring the stellar luminaries in the field of quantum physics: Bohr, Schrödinger, Einstein, Plank, and many others of the First Rank.

Both GPT and Claude do well throughout the book and particularly well when they pick up the quill and create a lively and multi-dimensional scene in Old Vienna. And I could not help myself: I asked them to work into the scene some dialog about Herr Schrödinger's cat, Fritz!

And you need to know that I was the maestro once again in this book, but I played none of the instruments. I only arranged the sheet music. I did not write the notes. But I did write this Introduction!

The entire text and supporting graphics were generated at my direction by using both GPT 4.o and Claude Sonnet 3.5 and Claude Pro.

You see my name, Herr Doctor Houze, only at the end, in summoning the creative gathering of the luminaries, Frau Annemarie (née Bertel) Schrödinger, and Fritz.

I hope you enjoy this book.

(01062025.v17)

Part A: The Birth and Evolution of an Idea: The Quantum State

Chapter 1: Quantum Foundations

Opening Narrative: "The Day Everything Changed"

On a day like any other, a group of scientists gathered in a dimly lit lab, surrounded by complex machinery and screens flickering with data. Little did they know, their work was about to unlock the doors to a realm of computing that defied classical understanding—a quantum revolution. This moment marked not just a leap in technology, but a shift in our very perception of reality and the nature of information itself.

Historical Context of Quantum Computing

The seeds of quantum computing were planted in the early 20th century, during a time of great scientific upheaval. Physicists were grappling with phenomena that classical physics could not explain, such as blackbody radiation and the photoelectric effect. These challenges required a new theoretical framework, leading to the birth of quantum mechanics.

Motivation Behind Early Quantum Theory

In the late 19th and early 20th centuries, several pivotal questions motivated scientists to challenge classical ideas:

Blackbody Radiation: Classical theories failed to explain the observed spectrum of electromagnetic radiation emitted by black bodies. Max Planck's resolution in 1900, proposing that energy is quantized, was a groundbreaking step towards quantum theory.

Photoelectric Effect: Albert Einstein's explanation in 1905, suggesting that light consists of particles called photons, was critical in establishing the particle wave duality, a cornerstone of quantum mechanics.

Atomic Structure: Niels Bohr's model of the atom in 1913, which incorporated quantized energy levels, provided a framework for understanding atomic stability and transitions.

Key Historical Milestones

1. Max Planck (1900): Introduced the concept of quantization of energy to solve the blackbody radiation problem, laying the groundwork for quantum theory.

2. Albert Einstein (1905): Explained the photoelectric effect, positing that light behaves as both a wave and a particle, which was crucial for the development of quantum mechanics.

3. Niels Bohr (1913): Developed the Bohr model of the atom, introducing the idea of quantized orbits for electrons. This model was a significant step in understanding atomic structure.

4. Werner Heisenberg (1927): Formulated the uncertainty principle, establishing fundamental limits on the precision with which certain pairs of physical properties can be known simultaneously.

5. Erwin Schrödinger (1926): Introduced the wave equation that describes how the quantum state of a physical system changes over time, leading to the development of wave mechanics.

These scientists were part of a vibrant intellectual community, often collaborating and debating ideas.

For example, the Solvay Conferences, starting in 1911, brought together leading physicists, including Einstein, Bohr, and Heisenberg, to discuss the implications of quantum theory.

Bridging to Modern Quantum Science

The work of early pioneers laid the foundation for later advancements in quantum mechanics and quantum computing. Key figures in the mid20th century and beyond have continued to bridge these ideas into practical applications:

Richard Feynman: In the 1980s, Feynman suggested that quantum systems could be simulated on quantum computers, marking a pivotal shift towards practical quantum computing.

David Deutsch: In 1985, Deutsch proposed the concept of a universal quantum computer, providing theoretical groundwork for quantum algorithms.

Nadia Nedjah and Mohamed AlRifaie: Their work in quantum algorithms and quantum programming languages has helped expand the toolkit for quantum computing, making it more accessible to researchers and developers.

Shafi Goldwasser and Silvio Micali: These two pioneering cryptographers made significant contributions to quantum cryptography, enhancing secure communication protocols that leverage quantum mechanics.

Women have also played crucial roles in advancing the field, such as:

Maria Goeppert Mayer: In 1963, she became the second woman to win the Nobel Prize in Physics for her work on the nuclear shell model, which has implications for quantum mechanics.

Chanda Prescod Weinstein: An astrophysicist and cosmologist, she has made contributions to quantum field theory and is an advocate for diversity in science.

Michelle Simmons: A leading researcher in quantum computing, she has worked on developing quantum bits using atomic scale technologies.

Evolution to Modern Quantum Computing

The journey from theoretical concepts to practical quantum computing involved numerous breakthroughs in both hardware and algorithms.

The late 20th and early 21st centuries saw the emergence of various quantum technologies, including superconducting qubits and ion traps, paving the way for the first experimental quantum computers.

Why Quantum Matters Now

In today's world, where data is generated at unprecedented rates, the limitations of classical computing have become apparent.

Quantum computing offers a new paradigm that promises to solve complex problems intractable for classical systems. Industries ranging from cryptography to drug discovery are poised to benefit from this technological advancement.

Computing Paradigm Shift

Quantum computing represents a fundamental shift in the way we process information. Unlike classical bits, which exist in binary states (0 or 1), qubits can exist in superpositions of states.

Analogy for Superposition: Imagine a spinning coin. While it's in the air, it isn't just heads or tails; it's in a state of both until it lands. Similarly, a qubit can hold a combination of both 0 and 1 at the same time until measured.

Technological Imperatives

As we stand on the brink of this quantum revolution, various technological imperatives drive research and development: Scalability: Creating scalable quantum systems capable of outperforming classical computers.

Error Correction: Developing robust error correction methods to mitigate the impact of decoherence and noise. Integration: Facilitating the integration of quantum systems with existing classical infrastructures.

Societal Impact

The impact of quantum computing extends beyond technology; it has the potential to reshape industries, economies, and even aspects of daily life.

From revolutionizing healthcare through advanced simulations to enhancing cybersecurity with quantum encryption, the societal implications are profound.

Advantages of Quantum Computation

- Superposition: Qubits can represent multiple states simultaneously, vastly increasing computational power.

- Entanglement: The phenomenon of entangled qubits allows for instantaneous information sharing, enhancing communication and computation.

Metaphor for Entanglement: Picture a pair of gloves. If you have one glove in one location and the other in a different location, knowing the state of one glove instantly tells you the state of the other, no matter the distance.

In quantum mechanics, entangled qubits behave similarly—changes to one qubit affect its entangled partner, regardless of the distance separating them.

3. Quantum Parallelism: Quantum algorithms can process a multitude of possibilities at once, providing significant speed advantages for specific tasks.

Insight Box: Future Impact

As we look ahead, the full potential of quantum computing remains largely untapped.

Innovations in quantum algorithms, error correction, and hardware will continue to drive progress.

The future may hold breakthroughs that transform industries in ways we can only begin to imagine.

Visual Aids

Quantum State Representation

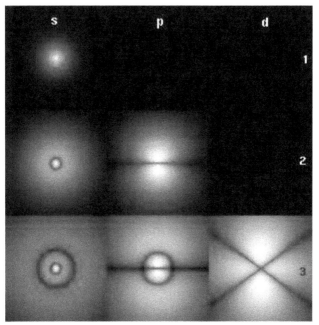

Timeline of Key Quantum Theory Historical Milestones: Create a visual timeline highlighting the contributions of Planck, Einstein, Bohr, Heisenberg, Schrödinger, and contemporary scientists that brought us to today's quantum computing.[1]

---

[11] https://www.talkerian.com/science/timeline-of-quantum-theories/
"TIMELINE OF QUANTUM COMPUTERS AND THE HISTORY OF QUANTUM COMPUTING." http://quantumly.com/timeline-of-quantum-computing-history-of-quantum-computers-dates.html. Timeline of quantum mechanics - Wikipedia

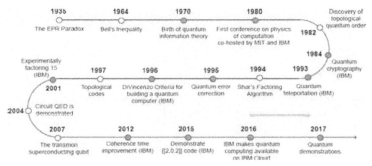

Bibliographic Material

Einstein, Albert. "On a Heuristic Viewpoint Concerning the Production and Transformation of Light." Annalen der Physik, 1905.[2]
[Link](https://www.researchgate.net/publication/258424717_On_a_Heuristic_Viewpoint_Concerning_the_Production_and_Transformation_of_Light)

Planck, Max. "On the Law of Distribution of Energy in the Normal Spectrum." Annalen der Physik, 1901.
[Link](https://www.researchgate.net/publication/258424731_On_the_Law_of_Distribution_of_Energy_in_the_Normal_Spectrum)

Bohr, Niels. "On the Constitution of Atoms and Molecules." Philosophical Magazine, 1913.

---

[2] See:
https://www.researchgate.net/publication/258424717_Tu_Z_Rigidity_of_proper_holomorphic_mappings_between_equidimensional_bounded_symmetric_domains_Proc_Am_Math_Soc_1304_1035-1042

[Link](https://www.researchgate.net/publication/258426165_On_the_Constitution_of_Atoms_and_Molecules)

Heisenberg, Werner. "Über den anschaulichen Inhalt der quantentheoretischen Kinematik und Mechanik." Zeitschrift für Physik, 1927.

Schrödinger in 1933

Chapter 2: Understanding Qubits

Quantum States and Measurement Theory

At the heart of quantum computing lies the concept of the qubit, or quantum bit, which is the basic unit of quantum information. Unlike classical bits that can be either 0 or 1, qubits can exist in a state of superposition, allowing them to represent both values simultaneously.

Analogy for Quantum States: Think of a qubit like a light switch that can be in an "off" position (0), an "on" position (1), or anywhere in between (superposition).

When the switch is flipped, the light can shine in varying degrees, illustrating how a qubit can represent multiple states at once.

Below is an illustration of the Quantum State in three sections.

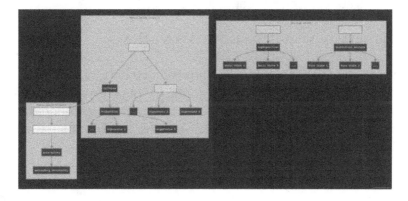

Source: Anthropic's Claude Sonnet 3.5

The Quantum State section, illustrating:

- Pure states and their superposition properties
- Mixed states and their statistical nature

The Measurement Process section, showing:

- How observables interact with quantum states
- The collapse mechanism

- Probabilistic outcomes

The Measurement Effects section, depicting:

- The wavefunction collapse process
- Post-measurement state characteristics
- Connection to uncertainty principles

Qubit State Vectors

In quantum mechanics, the state of a qubit is represented mathematically by a vector in a complex vector space.

A single qubit can be expressed as a linear combination of its basis states, typically denoted as:

$|0\rangle$ and $|1\rangle$: $$|\psi\rangle = \alpha |0\rangle + \beta |1\rangle$$

Here, α and β are complex numbers that define the probability amplitudes of measuring the qubit in either state. The probabilities of each outcome are given by the squared magnitudes of these amplitudes, satisfying the normalization condition:

$$|\alpha|^2 + |\beta|^2 = 1$$

Density Matrices

While state vectors provide a clear description of pure states, density matrices offer a more general representation that can describe both pure and mixed states.

A density matrix ρ is defined for a qubit as:

$$\rho = |\psi\rangle\langle\psi| = \begin{pmatrix} |\alpha|^2 & \alpha \beta^\wedge \\ \alpha^\wedge \beta & |\beta|^2 \end{pmatrix}$$

This formalism is particularly useful when considering systems that are entangled or when dealing with decoherence.

Quantum Measurement Fundamentals

Measurement in quantum mechanics is a unique process that alters the state of the system.

When a qubit is measured, it collapses from its superposition state to one of its basis states, 0 or 1, with probabilities defined by its state vector.

Types of Measurements

1. Projective Measurements: The standard method of measuring a qubit involves projecting its state onto one of the basis states. For example, measuring a qubit in the $|0\rangle$ and $|1\rangle$ basis will yield either 0 or 1, collapsing the superposition into one of the two possible outcomes.

2. Weak Measurements: These measurements provide probabilistic information about a qubit's state without fully collapsing it. They allow for the extraction of some information while retaining some degree of the qubit's original state.

3. Quantum State Tomography: A technique used to reconstruct the complete quantum state of a system by performing a series of projective measurements in different bases. This process gathers enough information to create a comprehensive picture of the qubit's state.

How Measurements are Made

Preparation: The qubit is initialized in a superposition state, often achieved using quantum gates that manipulate its quantum state.

Measurement Apparatus: Quantum measurements typically involve devices like superconducting circuits, ion traps, or photonic detectors, depending on the qubit implementation.

Measurement: An observational process is performed, causing the qubit to collapse to a definite state.

Outcome: The result is recorded, and the system is altered.

Metaphor for Measurement: Imagine a spinning coin. While it spins, it represents both heads and tails (superposition).

However, when you catch it, it lands on either heads or tails (measurement), and its state is determined.

Role of Classical Computers

Classical computers play a crucial role in quantum computing, particularly in the following ways:

1. Control and Calibration: Classical computers are used to control the quantum system, calibrate measurements, and ensure that the qubits are prepared in the desired states.

2. Data Processing: After measurements are made, classical computers process the results, performing complex calculations and algorithms that utilize the information obtained from the quantum system.

3. Hybrid Systems: Many quantum computing architectures operate in hybrid modes, where classical and quantum processors work in tandem. Classical computers handle

tasks that are more efficiently executed in a classical framework, such as error correction and data management.

4. Simulation and Algorithms: Classical computers are often employed to simulate quantum algorithms and to test quantum software before deploying it on actual quantum hardware.

Decoherence and Error Sources

Decoherence is a process that leads to the loss of quantum information due to interactions with the environment. It poses significant challenges for building reliable quantum computers. Key factors contributing to decoherence include:

Environmental Interactions: Noise from external systems can disrupt the delicate state of qubits.
Coherence Times: The duration for which a qubit maintains its quantum state before decohering is critical for successful quantum computation.

Error Mechanisms

Various errors can arise in quantum computing, including:

Bit-flip Errors: Occur when a qubit's state flips from 0 to 1 or vice versa.

Phase-flip Errors: Involve changes in the relative phase between the states of a qubit.

Depolarizing Noise: Random errors that affect the qubit state, causing it to lose its quantum information.
Key Analogies and Metaphors

To facilitate understanding, consider the following:

Superposition: Like a spinning coin representing both heads and tails.

Measurement: Catching the coin to reveal a definite outcome.

Entanglement: A pair of gloves where knowing the state of one instantly reveals the state of the other.

Clarifying Terminology

In this chapter, we have introduced several key terms related to quantum computing. Here's a brief clarification of some of them:

Qubit: The basic unit of quantum information, capable of existing in superposition.

Superposition: A state where a qubit can represent multiple values simultaneously.

Entanglement: A phenomenon where qubits become interconnected, such that the state of one qubit can instantaneously affect another, regardless of distance.

Decoherence: The loss of quantum coherence due to interactions with the environment.

Bibliographic Material

Nielsen, M. A., & Chuang, I. L. (2010). Quantum Computation and Quantum Information. Cambridge University Press.

Preskill, J. (2018). "Quantum Computing in the NISQ era and beyond." Quantum, 2, 79.

[Link](https://quantumjournal.org/papers/q2018080679/)

Mermin, N. D. (1993). Quantum Mechanics: Fixing the Measurement Problem. Physics Today, 46(7), 3847. [Link](https://aapt.scitation.org/doi/10.1119/1.17431)

Chapter 3: Quantum Logic Gates

Core Principles of Quantum Gates

Quantum gates are the fundamental building blocks of quantum circuits, much like classical logic gates are the building blocks of traditional computing. They manipulate qubits through various operations, enabling the execution of quantum algorithms.

Basic Quantum Gates

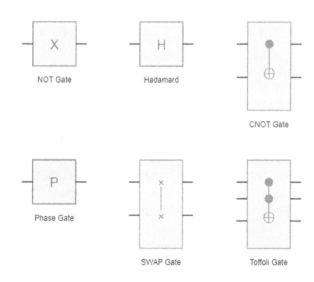

Source: Anthropic's Claude Sonnet Pro

Quantum Gate Details

1. X Gate (NOT Gate): Similar to the classical NOT gate, it flips the state of a qubit. Represented by an "X" in a blue box.
2. Hadamard (H) Gate: One of the most important quantum gates, it creates superposition by putting a qubit in an equal superposition of $|0\rangle$ and $|1\rangle$ states. Shown in orange.
3. CNOT Gate: A two-qubit gate where one qubit controls whether to apply an X gate to another qubit. Illustrated with a control point (dot) and target ($\oplus$).
4. Phase Gate (P): Adds a phase difference between $|0\rangle$ and $|1\rangle$ states. Shown in red.
5. SWAP Gate: Exchanges the states of two qubits. Represented by two crossed lines.
6. Toffoli Gate: A three-qubit gate with two control qubits and one target. Also known as CCNOT (Controlled-Controlled-NOT).

Each gate is color-coded for clarity, with input and output lines shown.

Analogy for Quantum Gates: Imagine a chef in a kitchen using different cooking techniques (chopping, boiling, baking) to prepare a meal. Each technique represents a different quantum gate, and the ingredients are the qubits.

By applying various techniques, the chef creates a unique dish, just as a quantum computer creates solutions to complex problems through the manipulation of qubits.

Unitary Operations: Quantum gates are represented by unitary matrices, which preserve the total probability. This means that the operation of a quantum gate can be reversed, much like how a well written recipe can be followed in reverse to recreate the original ingredients.

Superposition Manipulation: Quantum gates allow for the manipulation of qubits so they can exist in superposition states. This is akin to a musician playing multiple notes simultaneously and creating a rich harmony.

Entanglement: Some quantum gates can create entangled states, linking qubits in ways that enable complex quantum operations. Think of entangled qubits as a pair of dancers who move in perfect synchrony, where knowing the position of one dancer immediately reveals the position of the other.

Single Qubit Operations

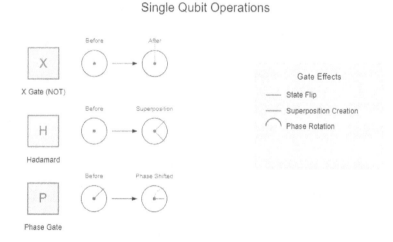

Source: Anthropic Claude Pro

Illustration Explanatory Details

This illustration shows three fundamental single qubit operations and their effects on quantum states:

1. X Gate (NOT Gate):

- o Represented in blue
- o Flips the state of a qubit from |0⟩ to |1⟩ or vice versa
- o Shown with a simple state transition
2. Hadamard (H) Gate:
  - o Represented in orange
  - o Creates superposition by transforming a basis state into an equal superposition
  - o Visualized with splitting arrows to represent superposition
3. Phase Gate (P):
  - o Represented in red
  - o Adds a phase difference to the qubit state
  - o Shown with a curved arrow indicating rotation in the phase space

The illustration includes:
- Clear gate symbols
- Before and after states
- Visual representations of the transformations
- A legend explaining the different types of operations

More Detail on Single Qubit Gates

Single qubit operations are the simplest type of quantum gates, acting on individual qubits. The most common single qubit gates include:

1. Pauli-X Gate (NOT Gate): This gate flips the state of a qubit from |0⟩ to |1⟩ and vice versa.

Example: Imagine flipping a switch. If the light is off (0), flipping the switch turns it on (1), and vice versa.

Its matrix representation is:

$$ X = \begin{pmatrix} 0 & 1 \\ 1 & 0 \end{pmatrix} $$

2. Pauli-Y Gate: This gate combines a Bit-flip and a phase flip operation.

Example: Picture a spinning top that can switch between rotating clockwise (1) and counterclockwise (0) while also adding a twist to its rotation.

Its matrix is represented as:

$$Y = \begin{pmatrix} 0 & i \\ i & 0 \end{pmatrix}$$

3. Pauli-Z Gate: This gate applies a phase shift to the $|1\rangle$ state without changing the $|0\rangle$ state.

Metaphor: Think of this gate as an artist who adds a filter to a photo, altering the appearance of the image without changing the subject itself.

Its matrix is:

$$Z = \begin{pmatrix} 1 & 0 \\ 0 & 1 \end{pmatrix}$$

4. Hadamard Gate (H Gate): This gate creates superposition, transforming

$|0\rangle$ into $\frac{1}{\sqrt{2}}(|0\rangle + |1\rangle)$ and $|1\rangle$

into

$\frac{1}{\sqrt{2}}(|0\rangle |1\rangle)$.

Illustration: Imagine a coin toss that can land on both heads and tails at once while it's in the air. The Hadamard gate sets up this scenario of uncertainty.

Its matrix representation is:

$$H = \begin{pmatrix} \frac{1}{\sqrt{2}} & \frac{1}{\sqrt{2}} \\ \frac{1}{\sqrt{2}} & \frac{1}{\sqrt{2}} \end{pmatrix}$$

Two Qubit Gates

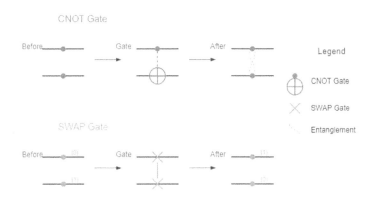

Source: Anthropic's Claude Pro

Two Qubit Gates Illustration: Explanatory Detail

This illustration shows two fundamental two-qubit gates and their operations:

1. CNOT Gate (Controlled-NOT):
   - Shows a control qubit (top) and target qubit (bottom)
   - The control qubit determines whether the target qubit is flipped
   - Demonstrates how entanglement is created between the two qubits
   - Indicated by the dashed lines connecting the qubits in the "After" state
2. SWAP Gate:
   - Exchanges the states of two qubits

28

- Represented by two × symbols connected by a vertical line
- Shows a clear before and after state with |0⟩ and |1⟩ labels
- Demonstrates how the qubit states are exchanged

The illustration includes:
- Before, during (gate), and after states for each operation
- Clear gate symbols and their effects
- A legend explaining the symbols used
- Visual representation of entanglement
- Color coding to distinguish different gates and their effects

More Detail on Two Qubit Gate Operational Principles

Two qubit gates operate on pairs of qubits and are crucial for creating entanglement.

Key examples include:

1. CNOT Gate (Controlled Not Gate): This gate flips the second qubit (target) if the first qubit (control) is in the |1⟩ state.

Mini Case Study: Imagine a light switch (control) that, when turned on, activates a fan (target). If the switch is off, the fan still remains. This interaction illustrates how the CNOT gate functions.

Its matrix representation is:

$$ \text{CNOT} = \begin{pmatrix} 1 & 0 & 0 & 0 \\ 0 & 1 & 0 & 0 \\ 0 & 0 & 0 & 1 \\ 0 & 0 & 1 & 0 \end{pmatrix} $$

2. SWAP Gate: This gate exchanges the states of two qubits.

Analogy: Think of two people swapping seats in a classroom. Each person moves to the other's position, just as the SWAP gate swaps the states of qubits.

Its matrix is:

$$\text{SWAP} = \begin{pmatrix} 1 & 0 & 0 & 0 \\ 0 & 0 & 1 & 0 \\ 0 & 1 & 0 & 0 \\ 0 & 0 & 0 & 1 \end{pmatrix}$$

Universal Gate Sets

A universal set of quantum gates can approximate any quantum operation to any desired level of accuracy. The combination of single qubit gates and the CNOT gate constitutes a universal gate set.

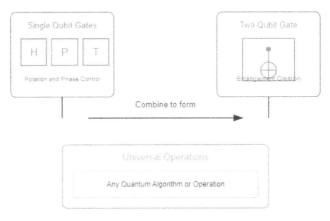

Universal Quantum Gate Set

• H: Hadamard gate (creates superposition)• P: Phase gate (controls phase)• T: π/8 gate (fine rotation control)

Source: Anthropic's Claude Pro

Illustration Explanatory Detail: Universal Quantum Gate Set

This illustration shows how universal gate sets work in quantum computing. The diagram is organized into three main sections:

1. Single Qubit Gates (Blue Section):
   o Shows the essential single-qubit gates: H (Hadamard), P (Phase), and T ($\pi/8$)
   o These gates handle rotation and phase control of individual qubits
2. Two-Qubit Gate (Red Section):
   o Features the CNOT gate as the essential two-qubit operation
   o Responsible for creating entanglement between qubits
3. Universal Operations (Green Section):
   o Shows how combining these basic gates enables any quantum operation
   o Represents the universality principle: these gates can approximate any quantum operation

The illustration includes:
- Clear grouping of gate types
- Flow showing how gates combine
- A legend explaining the purpose of each gate
- Color coding to distinguish different gate types and their roles

Metaphor: Consider a chef with a complete set of kitchen tools. With the right combination of knives, pots, and pans, the chef can create any dish imaginable, much like how a universal gate set enables the execution of any quantum algorithm.

Quantum Error Correction Fundamentals

Quantum Error Correction Fundamentals

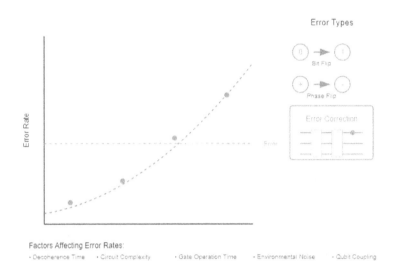

Source: Anthropic's Claude Pro

Explanatory Notes: Illustration of Quantum Error Correction Fundamentals

This is a comprehensive illustration of quantum error correction fundamentals that includes:

1. Main Scatter Plot:
    - Shows the relationship between time/complexity and error rates
    - Red dashed line shows error growth without correction
    - Green threshold line indicates the maximum acceptable error rate
    - Blue data points show error measurements at different stages
2. Error Types Section:

        ○   Bit Flip: Shows the $|0\rangle$ to $|1\rangle$ transition
        ○   Phase Flip: Shows the $|+\rangle$ to $|-\rangle$ transition
        ○   Simplified correction circuit showing basic error detection and correction

3. Key Factors Affecting Error Rates:
        ○   Decoherence time
        ○   Circuit complexity
        ○   Gate operation time
        ○   Environmental noise
        ○   Qubit coupling

The visualization emphasizes:

- The critical threshold for error correction
- Different types of quantum errors
- The relationship between complexity and error rates
- Basic correction mechanisms

More Detail on Quantum Error Correction

Quantum error correction is essential for maintaining the integrity of quantum information, as qubits are prone to errors due to decoherence and noise. Key concepts include:

1. Quantum Error Correcting Codes: These codes protect quantum information by encoding it across multiple qubits.

Example: The Shor Code encodes one logical qubit into nine physical qubits, much like a backup system that spreads data across multiple drives to prevent loss.

2. Fault Tolerance: This concept refers to the ability of quantum algorithms to continue functioning correctly even in the presence of errors.

Analogy: Think of a car designed to keep running smoothly despite a flat tire. It uses spare tires and mechanisms to compensate for faults.

3. Threshold Theorem: This theorem states that as long as the error rate is below a certain threshold, arbitrary long quantum computations can be performed reliably using error correcting codes.

Error Types and Sources

Various errors can arise in quantum computing, including:

Bit-flip Errors: Occur when a qubit's state flips from 0 to 1 or vice versa.

Analogy: This is like accidentally flipping a light switch when you meant to adjust the thermostat.

Phase-flip Errors: Involve changes in the relative phase between the states of a qubit.

Example: Think of this as a musician who accidentally plays a note at the wrong time in a symphony, throwing off the harmony.

Depolarizing Noise: Random errors that affect the qubit state, causing it to lose its quantum information.

Metaphor: Imagine trying to listen to a radio station with poor reception—random static disrupts the clarity of the music.

Quantum Circuit Implementation

Quantum circuits are constructed by arranging quantum gates to perform specific operations. The design of quantum circuits involves:

Circuit Design Principles: Understanding how to arrange gates to achieve desired operations while minimizing errors—similar to laying out a blueprint for a building.

Optimization Techniques: Strategies to reduce the number of gates or depth of the circuit, enhancing performance and efficiency—like streamlining a recipe to save time and ingredients.

Hardware Constraints: Considerations related to the physical implementation of qubits, such as coherence times and error rates, are crucial for effective quantum computing.

Case Studies

1. IBM Quantum Experience: IBM has developed a cloud based quantum computing platform that allows researchers and developers to run quantum algorithms on real quantum hardware. Users can experiment with different quantum circuits and algorithms, learning about quantum mechanics hands on.

2. Google Quantum AI: Google's quantum computing initiative focuses on developing quantum processors and algorithms, achieving significant milestones, such as demonstrating quantum supremacy. Their research showcases the practical applications of quantum gates in solving complex problems.

3. Rigetti Computing: This company is working on building quantum processors and providing access to quantum computing via the cloud, emphasizing hybrid quantum classical computing. Their efforts illustrate how quantum gates can be integrated into larger computing frameworks.

Visual Aids

Diagram of Quantum Gates: The first diagram depicts the operations of single qubit quantum gates; the second diagram depicts the operations of multiple qubit logic gates.

Single-Qubit Quantum Gates

X Gate (NOT)	H Gate (Hadamard)	Z Gate (Phase)
$|0\rangle \rightarrow |1\rangle$	$|0\rangle \rightarrow (|0\rangle + |1\rangle)/\sqrt{2}$	$|0\rangle \rightarrow |0\rangle$
$|1\rangle \rightarrow |0\rangle$	$|1\rangle \rightarrow (|0\rangle - |1\rangle)/\sqrt{2}$	$|1\rangle \rightarrow -|1\rangle$

S Gate	T Gate	Y Gate
$\pi/2$ phase rotation	$\pi/4$ phase rotation	iXZ rotation

Source: Anthropic's Claude Pro

Explanatory Notes:

The first diagram shows single-qubit gates, organized into two rows:
- Primary gates (X, Hadamard, and Z) with their basic state transformations
- Phase gates (S, T, and Y) with their rotation properties

Multi-Qubit Quantum Gates

CNOT Gate
Control Qubit: $|1\rangle$
Target: NOT operation
$|10\rangle \rightarrow |11\rangle, |11\rangle \rightarrow |10\rangle$

SWAP Gate
Exchanges two qubits:
$|01\rangle \rightarrow |10\rangle$
$|00\rangle$ and $|11\rangle$ unchanged

Controlled-Z Gate
Control Qubit: $|1\rangle$
Target: Phase flip
$|11\rangle \rightarrow -|11\rangle$

Controlled-Phase Gate
Control Qubit: $|1\rangle$
Target: Phase rotation
$|11\rangle \rightarrow e^{i\varphi}|11\rangle$

Source: Anthropic's Claude Pro

Explanatory Notes:

1. The second diagram shows multi-qubit gates:

    o   CNOT and SWAP gates in the top row

    o   Controlled-Z and Controlled-Phase gates in the bottom row

Each gate is presented in a clear, boxed format with:

- The gate name and common alternate name

- Basic operation description

- State transformations in standard bra-ket notation

The diagrams use a consistent color scheme:

- Light blue for single-qubit gates

- Warm orange for multi-qubit gates

- Clear typography and spacing for optimal readability

Quantum Circuit Example: The simplified diagram shows the arrangement of gates to perform a specific operation.

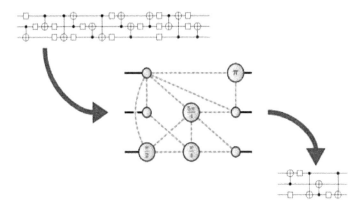

Bibliographic Material

Nielsen, M. A., & Chuang, I. L. (2010). Quantum Computation and Quantum Information. Cambridge University Press.

Shor, P. W. (1994). "Algorithms for Quantum Computation: Discrete Logarithms and Factoring." Proceedings of the 35th Annual ACM Symposium on Theory of Computing, 124134.

Gottesman, D. (1997). "Stabilizer Codes and Quantum Error Correction." California Institute of Technology. [Link](https://arxiv.org/abs/quantph/9705052)

Chapter 4: Quantum Algorithms

Introduction to Quantum Algorithms

Quantum algorithms leverage the principles of quantum mechanics to solve complex problems more efficiently than classical algorithms. They take advantage of superposition, entanglement, and interference to process information in innovative ways.

The successful development and deployment of these algorithms require a diverse team with expertise across various domains.

Metaphor for Quantum Algorithms: Imagine a massive library filled with countless books (data).

A classical computer is like a librarian who must search through each book one by one, while a quantum algorithm acts as a magical librarian who can read multiple books simultaneously, finding the desired information much faster.

The Team Composition for Quantum Algorithm Development

The process of developing quantum algorithms involves a collaborative effort from multiple disciplines.

Each team member contributes unique skills and perspectives, ensuring that all aspects of the algorithm's lifecycle are addressed effectively.

1. Mathematicians:

Role: Mathematicians are essential for formulating the theoretical foundations of quantum algorithms. They use advanced mathematical concepts, such as linear algebra, probability theory, and number theory, to develop and analyze algorithms.

Example: A mathematician might analyze the efficiency of Shor's algorithm in factoring large integers, ensuring its viability for practical applications.

2. Physicists:

Role: Quantum physicists provide insights into the principles of quantum mechanics that underpin quantum computing. Their expertise is critical in understanding qubit behavior, decoherence, and the physical implementation of quantum systems.

Analogy: Think of physicists as architects who design the framework of a building based on the laws of physics, ensuring that it can withstand environmental forces.

3. Computer Scientists:

Role: Computer scientists design the infrastructure and algorithms needed to implement quantum computing solutions.

They focus on optimizing algorithms, managing data, and ensuring that the algorithms can run efficiently on quantum hardware.

Illustration: Picture computer scientists as engineers who build the roads and bridges necessary for transportation, ensuring that the flow of traffic (data) is smooth and efficient.

4. Software Developers:

Role: Software developers write the code that implements quantum algorithms on quantum processors and classical systems. They create user interfaces, libraries, and frameworks that allow researchers and practitioners to access quantum capabilities.

Example: A software developer might work on a quantum programming language that simplifies the process of writing quantum algorithms, making them more accessible to a broader audience.

5. AI and Machine Learning Experts:

Role: AI specialists explore the intersection of quantum computing and artificial intelligence, designing algorithms that leverage quantum speedup for machine learning tasks. They help optimize quantum algorithms for data processing and pattern recognition.

Metaphor: AI experts are like chefs who experiment with new recipes, combining ingredients (quantum algorithms) to create innovative dishes (machine learning models) that are more effective than classical approaches.

6. Project Managers:

Role: Project managers oversee the development process, ensuring that the team stays on schedule and meets operational goals. They facilitate communication between team members, handle resource allocation, and manage stakeholder expectations.

Analogy: Consider project managers as conductors of an orchestra, ensuring that all musicians (team members) play in harmony and produce a cohesive performance.

The Development Process of Quantum Algorithms

The development of quantum algorithms involves several key stages, requiring collaboration among the diverse team members:

1. Problem Identification: The first step is defining the operational goal or problem that the algorithm will address. This often involves input from mathematicians, physicists,

and computer scientists to ensure a comprehensive understanding of the challenge.

Example: A team identifies the need for a faster algorithm to solve optimization problems in logistics, requiring expertise in both quantum mechanics and algorithm design.

2. Theoretical Development: Mathematicians and physicists collaborate to create a theoretical framework for the algorithm, outlining how it will function based on quantum principles.

Analogy: This stage resembles drafting a blueprint for a building, where the design must consider various structural elements and materials.

3. Algorithm Design: The team then designs the algorithm, determining the specific quantum gates and operations required. This stage involves close collaboration between computer scientists and software developers to ensure the algorithm can be implemented effectively.

Illustration: Imagine chefs working together in a kitchen, each responsible for different components of a dish, ensuring that all ingredients come together seamlessly.

4. Testing and Simulation: Before deploying the algorithm on quantum hardware, the team conducts extensive testing through simulations on classical computers. This step involves feedback from all team members to identify potential issues and areas for improvement.

Metaphor: This process is akin to a pilot testing a new airplane design in a flight simulator, allowing for adjustments before taking it to the skies.

5. Refinement: Based on the results of testing, the team refines the algorithm to enhance its efficiency and reliability. This iterative process may involve adjusting quantum gates, optimizing circuit design, and addressing error rates.

Mini Case Study: During testing, a researcher might discover that a specific quantum gate introduces excessive noise. The team collaborates to explore alternative gate configurations that yield a more stable outcome.

6. Deployment: After thorough testing and refinement, the algorithm is deployed on a quantum computer. This phase involves collaboration with software developers to ensure that the algorithm integrates smoothly with existing quantum programming frameworks.

Illustration: The deployment stage is like launching a new product after months of development, where the team ensures that everything is ready for users.

The Importance of Classical and Quantum Collaboration

The integration of classical and quantum computing is essential for the successful development and application of quantum algorithms.

While quantum computers excel at specific tasks, classical computers remain invaluable for many traditional computations.

1. Hybrid Approach: Many modern quantum algorithms leverage hybrid approaches, where classical systems handle preprocessing, error correction, and data management while quantum systems perform complex calculations.

Example: In quantum machine learning, classical algorithms preprocess data, while quantum algorithms run specific models to enhance performance, combining the strengths of both realms.

2. Feedback Loops: The relationship between classical and quantum computing is iterative, with results from quantum computations needing to be interpreted and refined using classical algorithms. This collaboration enhances overall performance.

Illustration: Think of a scientific experiment where initial results lead to further classical analysis, which inspires new quantum tests, continuously refining the understanding of the problem.

Notable Quantum Algorithms and Their Applications

While previously discussed algorithms like Shor's and Grover's are well known, several others are also critical, each suited to specific tasks:

1. Quantum Phase Estimation: This algorithm determines the eigenvalues of a unitary operator, forming a basis for many other quantum algorithms, particularly in quantum simulations and optimization problems.

2. Variational Quantum Eigensolver (VQE): VQE is used to find the lowest eigenstate of a Hamiltonian, making it valuable for quantum chemistry and materials science. This algorithm combines classical optimization with quantum circuit evaluations, showcasing the hybrid nature of quantum computing.

3. Quantum Approximate Optimization Algorithm (QAOA): QAOA tackles combinatorial optimization problems by applying variational techniques. It is particularly useful for problems like the traveling salesman and Max Cut problem.

4. Quantum Walks: Quantum walks are used for search algorithms and optimization problems, leveraging the principles of quantum superposition and interference to explore graph structures more efficiently than classical random walks.

5. Quantum Machine Learning Algorithms: These algorithms, like Quantum Support Vector Machines and Quantum Neural Networks, combine quantum computing with machine learning principles to enhance data processing and pattern recognition.

The Evolution of Classical and Quantum Relationships

The relationship between classical and quantum computing has evolved significantly over the years:

Early Days: Initially, quantum computing was purely theoretical, with researchers exploring quantum principles without practical applications.

Development of Quantum Algorithms: The introduction of algorithms like Shor's and Grover's marked a turning point, demonstrating the potential of quantum computing to outperform classical methods.

Hybrid Models: As quantum hardware developed, the focus shifted to hybrid models that leverage the strengths of both classical and quantum systems, leading to practical applications across various fields.

Current Landscape: Today, the collaboration between classical and quantum computing is at the forefront of research, with ongoing efforts to create more efficient algorithms and robust quantum hardware.

Conclusion

Quantum algorithms represent a significant advancement in computational capabilities, particularly when integrated with classical systems.

The interdisciplinary nature of the development process, involving mathematicians, physicists, computer scientists, software developers, and AI experts, underscores the importance of collaboration in achieving innovative solutions.

By harnessing the strengths of both classical and quantum computing, researchers can tackle complex problems more efficiently and effectively, paving the way for transformative advancements in technology.

Visual Aids

Team Composition Diagram: Illustrate the roles and contributions of different team members in the development of quantum algorithms.

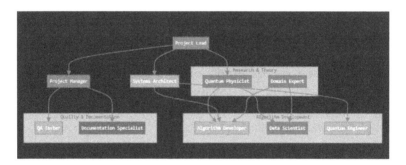

Source: Anthropic's Claude Sonnet 3.5

Leadership Roles (Red):
  1. Project Lead: Provides overall direction and strategic oversight

2. Project Manager: Handles day-to-day coordination and resource management

Technical Roles (Green):
1. Quantum Engineer: Implements quantum circuits and handles hardware integration
2. Algorithm Developer: Translates theoretical concepts into practical implementations
3. QA Tester: Ensures algorithm reliability and performance
4. Systems Architect: Designs overall system architecture

Research Roles (Blue):
1. Quantum Physicist: Provides theoretical foundation and quantum mechanics expertise
2. Data Scientist: Analyzes algorithm performance and optimization
3. Domain Expert: Brings specific industry/application knowledge

Support Role (Purple):
1. Documentation Specialist: Maintains technical documentation and specifications

The diagram shows both hierarchical relationships and functional groupings.

The three main subgroups (Algorithm Development, Research & Theory, and Quality & Documentation) highlight how different roles collaborate on specific aspects of the development process.

Flowchart of Algorithm Development: Visualize the stages of conception, design, testing, refinement, and deployment of quantum algorithms.

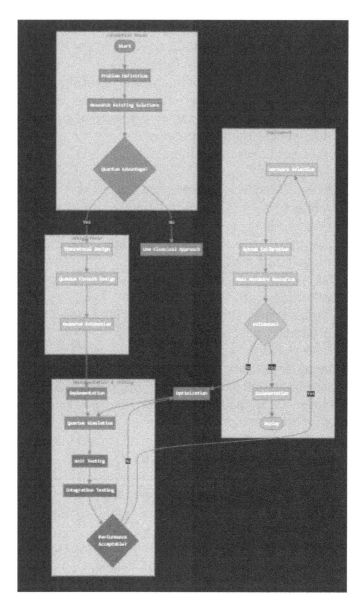

Source: Anthropic's Claude Sonnet 3.5

This comprehensive flowchart shows the full lifecycle of quantum algorithm development. The process is color-coded into five main phases:

Conception Phase (Red):
- Starts with problem definition
- Includes research of existing solutions
- Evaluates quantum advantage feasibility

Design Phase (Green):
- Theoretical design of the quantum algorithm
- Quantum circuit design
- Resource estimation and complexity analysis

Implementation Phase (Blue):
- Initial implementation
- Quantum simulation on classical computers
- Optimization cycles as needed

Testing Phase (Purple):
- Unit testing of components
- Integration testing
- Performance evaluation

Deployment Phase (Orange):
- Hardware selection and calibration
- Real hardware execution
- Final validation and documentation

Key Features of the Flowchart:
1. Multiple decision points that can trigger refinement loops
2. Clear feedback paths for optimization
3. Distinct separation between simulation and real hardware phases
4. Integration of both theoretical and practical considerations

Algorithm by Type Comparison Table[3]:

Here's a comparison table highlighting classical algorithms alongside their quantum counterparts, focusing on differences in efficiency and applications:

Classical Algorithm	Quantum Counterpart	Efficiency Improvement	Applications
Sorting Algorithms	Grover's Search	Quadratic speedup ($O(\sqrt{N})$ vs $O(N)$	Database search, optimization problems
Integer Factorization	Shor's Algorithm	Exponential speedup ($O(N^3)$ vs $O(\exp(N^{1/3})$	Cryptography (RSA encryption)
Search Algorithms	Grover's Algorithm	Quadratic speedup ($O(\sqrt{N})$ vs $O(N)$	Unstructured search
Simulation of Quantum Systems	Quantum Simulation	Polynomial speedup	Chemistry, materials science
Linear Algebra	HHL Algorithm	Exponential speedup in specific cases	($O(\log N)$) | Machine learning, optimization
Optimization Problems	Quantum Approximate Optimization Algorithm (QAOA)	Potentially better solutions in fewer iterations	Combinatorial optimization
Graph Algorithms	Quantum Walks	Potentially faster than classical	Network analysis, pathfinding

---

[3] Source for all tabular data in this book: GPT 4.0

Key Takeaways:

Efficiency Improvement: Quantum algorithms often provide significant improvements in time complexity for specific tasks, particularly in problems related to searching and factorization.

Applications: Quantum algorithms are particularly useful in areas such as cryptography, optimization, and simulations that are computationally intensive for classical computers.

This table highlights the transformative potential of quantum computing in various fields, emphasizing how quantum algorithms can outperform classical ones under certain conditions.

Bibliographic Material

Nielsen, M. A., & Chuang, I. L. (2010). Quantum Computation and Quantum Information. Cambridge University Press.

Shor, P. W. (1994). "Algorithms for Quantum Computation: Discrete Logarithms and Factoring." Proceedings of the 35th Annual ACM Symposium on Theory of Computing, 124134.

Grover, L. K. (1996). "A Fast Quantum Mechanical Algorithm for Database Search." Proceedings of the 28th Annual ACM Symposium on Theory of Computing, 212219.

Chapter 5: Quantum Hardware

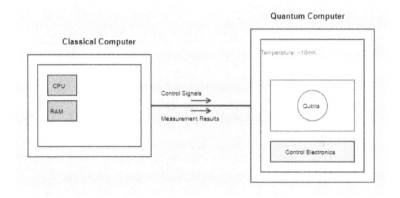

Source: Anthropic's Claude Sonnet 3.5

(This illustration depicts two actions that classical computers take to control the quantum computer)

Introduction to Quantum Hardware

Quantum hardware is the physical infrastructure that enables quantum computing, providing the necessary platform for executing quantum algorithms.

The effectiveness and design of quantum hardware are crucial for harnessing the full power of quantum computing, as they directly influence the performance, scalability, and reliability of quantum algorithms.

Metaphor for Quantum Hardware: Consider quantum hardware as the engine of a vehicle. Just as an engine drives a car and determines its speed and efficiency, quantum hardware powers quantum algorithms, impacting their execution and capabilities.

Types of Quantum Hardware

There are several leading approaches to building quantum hardware, each with unique advantages and challenges.

The most notable types include:

1. Superconducting Qubits:

Description: Superconducting qubits utilize superconducting circuits that function at extremely low temperatures. They exploit the Josephson effect to create and manipulate qubit states.

Examples: Major companies like IBM and Google have developed quantum processors using superconducting qubits, achieving impressive coherence times and gate speeds.

Analogy: Imagine superconducting qubits as finely tuned musical instruments, where precise environmental conditions (such as low temperatures) are essential for optimal performance.

2. Trapped Ions:

Description: This approach involves using electromagnetic fields to trap individual ions, which serve as qubits. Quantum operations are performed by directing laser beams to manipulate the states of these ions.

Examples: Companies such as IonQ and Honeywell have developed trapped ion quantum computers that demonstrate high fidelity and long coherence times, making them reliable for quantum computations.

Illustration: Visualize a skilled puppeteer controlling a set of marionettes (ions), where lasers act as strings guiding their movements in perfect synchronization.

3. Photonic Quantum Computing:

Description: Photonic systems utilize photons as qubits, manipulating them through optical components like beam splitters and wave plates. This approach is particularly advantageous for fast and robust quantum communication.

Examples: Xanadu and PsiQuantum are notable companies pioneering photonic quantum computing, focusing on its potential for quantum networking and secure communication.

Metaphor: Imagine a dazzling light show where each photon is a dancer, moving gracefully across the stage. The choreography (quantum gates) dictates how the dancers interact and form intricate patterns (quantum states).

4. Topological Qubits:

Description: Topological qubits are based on anyons—exotic particles that exist in two dimensional spaces.

Their unique topological properties promise inherent error resistance, making them a strong candidate for fault tolerant quantum computing.

Examples: Microsoft is actively researching topological qubits, aiming to develop a quantum computer that can withstand noise and errors in practical environments.

Analogy: Think of topological qubits as a sturdy ship designed to navigate turbulent seas (errors), where the ship's shape (topology) provides stability irrespective of the surrounding conditions.

Comparison of Classical Supercomputers and Quantum Computers

To better understand the differences between classical supercomputers and modern quantum computers, the following table summarizes key aspects of their hardware, operating systems, environmental requirements, energy consumption, and more.

Feature	Classical Supercomputer	Quantum Computer
Architecture	Based on classical bits (0s and 1s	Based on quantum bits (qubits) that can exist in superposition
Processing Model	Sequential and parallel processing using multiple cores	Quantum parallelism leveraging superposition and entanglement
Operating System	Traditional operating systems (e.g., Linux)	Specialized quantum programming frameworks (e.g., Qiskit, Cirq
Environmental Requirements	Standard operating conditions (room temperature)	Requires ultralow temperatures (close to absolute zero) for superconducting qubits or high vacuum for trapped ions

Energy Consumption	| High power consumption due to cooling and hardware demands	Potentially lower energy consumption for certain tasks, but currently requires significant energy for cooling and maintenance
Error Correction	Classical error correction techniques	Quantum error correction is complex and still under development
Scalability	Can be scaled with additional hardware	Scalability is challenging due to qubit coherence and error rates
Applications	General purpose computing, simulations, data analysis	Specific tasks like factoring, optimization, and quantum simulations

Here is a scatter plot visualization comparing classical supercomputers and quantum computers across multiple dimensions.

Classical Supercomputers vs. Quantum Computers

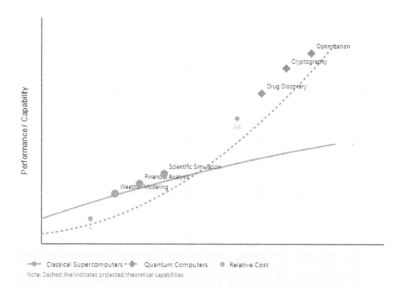

Illustration Explanatory Notes

This comprehensive scatter plot compares classical supercomputers and quantum computers across multiple dimensions:
1. Axes and Curves:
    o X-axis: Technology Maturity/Time
    o Y-axis: Performance/Capability
    o Solid blue line: Classical computing trajectory
    o Dashed red line: Quantum computing trajectory
2. Key Applications: Classical Computing (Blue circles):
    o Weather Modeling
    o Financial Analysis

- o   Scientific Simulation

Quantum Computing (Red squares):
- o   Drug Discovery
- o   Cryptography
- o   Optimization

3. Cost Indicators:
- o   Green circles with $ symbols showing relative costs
- o   Shows increasing cost trend for both technologies

4. Notable Features:
- o   Intersection point showing where quantum advantage might occur
- o   Steeper curve for quantum computing indicating potential exponential growth
- o   Clear separation of current vs. future applications

The visualization emphasizes:
- The different growth trajectories
- Current vs. future capabilities
- Cost implications
- Application domains
- Relative maturity of technologies

Operational Principles of Quantum Hardware

Quantum hardware operates on the fundamental principles of quantum mechanics.

The behavior of qubits, including superposition and entanglement, allows quantum computers to perform complex calculations that are infeasible for classical computers.

Superposition: Qubits can exist in multiple states simultaneously, enabling quantum computers to process vast amounts of information at once. This principle allows for parallel computation, significantly enhancing performance.

Entanglement: Entangled qubits exhibit correlations that transcend classical limitations, enabling faster and more efficient information transfer. This property is essential for many quantum algorithms, which rely on the intricate relationships between qubits.

Quantum Gates: Quantum hardware uses quantum gates to manipulate qubit states, similar to classical logic gates in traditional computing. These gates perform operations that change the probabilities of a qubit's state, allowing for complex quantum computations.

Challenges in Quantum Hardware Development

Despite the promising capabilities of quantum hardware, several challenges must be addressed:

1. Decoherence and Noise: Qubits are sensitive to their environment, and interactions with external factors can lead to decoherence, causing loss of quantum information. Minimizing noise and extending coherence times are critical for reliable quantum computations.

Metaphor: Imagine trying to listen to a symphony while surrounded by loud distractions. The ability to maintain focus (coherence) is crucial for capturing the beauty of the music (quantum states).

2. Scalability: Building largescale quantum computers that can effectively run complex algorithms is a significant challenge, as it requires a substantial number of qubits with high fidelity and low error rates.

Analogy: Consider constructing a massive skyscraper; the more floors (qubits) you need, the greater the challenge to ensure the building is stable and functional.

3. Integration with Classical Systems: Quantum hardware must work in tandem with classical computing systems, necessitating seamless integration to leverage the strengths of both technologies.

Illustration: Think of a relay race where each runner (classical and quantum systems) has specialized skills. Effective handoffs between runners are crucial for achieving the best overall performance.

The Relationship Between Quantum Hardware and Algorithms

The interplay between quantum hardware and algorithms is vital for the advancement of quantum computing. The capabilities of quantum hardware dictate the types of algorithms that can be implemented effectively. Conversely, advances in algorithm design can drive the development of improved hardware.

Feedback Loop: As quantum algorithms evolve, they provide insights into the requirements for quantum hardware, influencing design decisions and leading to enhancements in qubit technology and error correction methods.

Hybrid Approaches: Many quantum algorithms utilize hybrid models, where classical and quantum systems work together. Quantum hardware executes certain complex calculations, while classical systems manage preprocessing, error correction, and data handling.

Example: In quantum machine learning applications, classical algorithms preprocess data, while quantum algorithms enhance model performance, demonstrating the collaborative power of both realms.

Conclusion

Quantum hardware is foundational to the success of quantum algorithms, directly influencing their performance and scalability.

The diverse approaches to building quantum hardware each bring unique advantages and challenges, requiring ongoing research and development.

By understanding the operational principles of quantum hardware and its relationship with algorithms, researchers can continue to push the boundaries of quantum computing, unlocking new possibilities for solving complex problems across various fields.

Visual Aids

Diagram of Quantum Hardware Types[4]: Illustrate the various types of quantum hardware, along with their characteristics and examples of companies working within each category.

---

[4] Link to an overview of quantum computation hardware components:
https://www.researchgate.net/publication/376718664_The_Curren t_Landscape_of_Quantum_Hardware_Development_-An_Overview

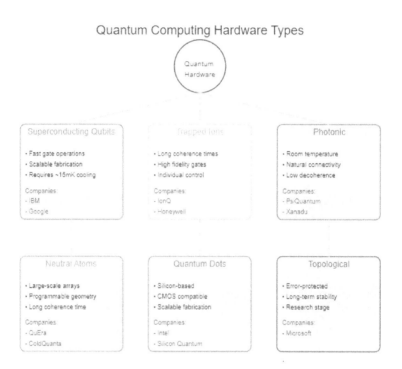

Source: Anthropic's Claude Pro

Explanatory Notes: Quantum Computer Hardware Types

This comprehensive diagram shows the main types of quantum computing hardware. The visualization includes:

1. Core Technologies:
   o Superconducting Qubits (Blue)
   o Trapped Ions (Yellow)
   o Photonic (Red)
   o Neutral Atoms (Green)
   o Quantum Dots (Light Blue)
   o Topological (Purple)
2. For each technology, the diagram shows:
   o Key characteristics
   o Operating requirements

- o Major companies working in the field
- o Current state of development
3. Notable Features:
    - o Color coding for different technologies
    - o Clear hierarchical structure
    - o Company associations
    - o Key technical characteristics

The diagram emphasizes:

- The diversity of quantum computing approaches
- Different maturity levels
- Various technical requirements
- Industry players in each category

This is an illustration of the foundational components of a quantum computer setup.

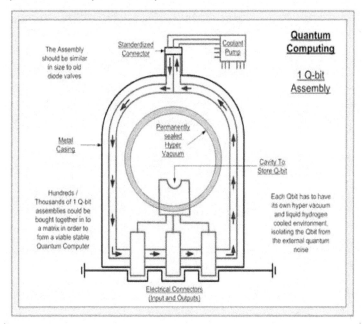

Quantum Computing, The Qbit Free Stock Photo - Public Domain Pictures
by Unknown Author

Comparison Table: This table displays both classical supercomputers and quantum computers, highlighting their high-level differences and similarities.

Feature	Classical Supercomputers	Quantum Computers
Architecture	Based on classical bits (0s and 1s)	Based on quantum bits (qubits)
Processing Power	High performance through parallel processing	Exponential processing power for specific tasks
Data Storage	Uses RAM and disk storage	Uses quantum states for information storage
Speed	Fast for solving deterministic problems	Potentially faster for problems like factoring and searching
Programming Model	Traditional programming languages (C, Fortran	Quantum programming languages (Qiskit, Q#)
Error Rates	Typically low error rates	Higher error rates; requires error correction
Applications	Weather modeling, simulations, big data analytics	Cryptography, optimization, quantum chemistry

Scalability	Scalable through adding more nodes	Challenges in scaling due to qubit coherence and error rates
Cost	High initial investment but widely available	Currently high due to technology limitations and development costs
Development Stage	Mature and widely used	Emerging technology with ongoing research
Similarities	High-Performance Computing	Both aim to solve complex problems beyond the reach of standard computers.
Research Applications	Both types of computers are used in research, albeit in different capacities and domains.	Both types of computers are used in research, albeit in different capacities and domains.

Key Takeaways:
- Classical supercomputers excel in tasks requiring large-scale computations with established algorithms, while quantum computers show promise in specific areas that can leverage their unique properties, such as superposition and entanglement.

- The two technologies are not directly competing but rather complement each other, with quantum computers potentially handling problems that are currently infeasible for classical systems.

Operational Principles Flowchart[5]: Visualize the key principles of quantum hardware and how they contribute to quantum computation.

https://www.mymap.ai/share/quantum-data-transmission-process-flow-chart-bzrszzkApHvFx

Integration Model: The link below shows the interaction between quantum hardware and classical systems in a hybrid computing environment.

https://www.researchgate.net/figure/Schematic-of-a-hybrid-quantum-classical-computing-architecture_fig1_320196037

Bibliographic Material

Nielsen, M. A., & Chuang, I. L. (2010). Quantum Computation and Quantum Information. Cambridge University Press.

---

[5] "Visualize Quantum Circuits with Q# - Azure Quantum." 23 Oct. 2024, https://learn.microsoft.com/en-us/azure/quantum/how-to-visualize-circuits.
"Quantum Gates and Circuits: The Building Blocks of Quantum Computation." https://quantumzeitgeist.com/quantum-gates-and-circuits/.
"Quantum Circuit Diagram Conventions - Azure Quantum | Microsoft Learn." 16 Sept. 2024, https://learn.microsoft.com/en-us/azure/quantum/concepts-circuits.
"Quantum computing: A taxonomy, systematic review and future directions ...."
https://onlinelibrary.wiley.com/doi/10.1002/spe.3039.

Preskill, J. (2018). "Quantum Computing in the NISQ era and beyond." Quantum, 2, 79.

[Link](https://quantumjournal.org/papers/q2018080679/)
Devoret, M. H., & Schoelkopf, R. J. (2013). "Superconducting Qubits: A Short Review." Science, 339(6124), 11691174.

Chapter 6: Quantum Applications

Introduction to Quantum Applications

Quantum computing holds the promise of revolutionizing various fields by solving complex problems that are intractable for classical computers.

As quantum technology matures, its applications are expanding across multiple industries, offering unprecedented opportunities for innovation and efficiency.

Classical vs Quantum Computing: Cost-Benefit Analysis

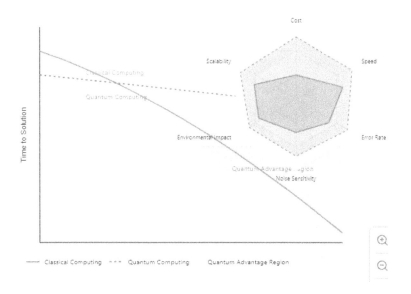

Source: Anthropic's Claude Pro

Explanatory Notes: Classical vs Quantum Computing: Cost-Benefit Analysis

This is a comprehensive visualization comparing classical and quantum computing across multiple dimensions:

1. Main Plot Area:
    - X-axis: Problem Complexity (number of variables)
    - Y-axis: Time to Solution
    - Shows exponential growth for classical computing
    - Shows polynomial growth for quantum computing
    - Highlights the "Quantum Advantage Region" where quantum computers outperform classical ones
2. Radar Chart Metrics: Cost:

- Classical: Lower initial but scales up
- Quantum: Higher initial investment

Speed:
- Classical: Linear to exponential scaling
- Quantum: Potential exponential speedup for specific problems

Error Rate:
- Classical: Very low
- Quantum: Currently high, improving with technology

Noise Sensitivity:
- Classical: Low
- Quantum: High, requires significant error correction

Environmental Impact:
- Classical: Moderate energy usage
- Quantum: High cooling requirements

Scalability:
- Classical: Well-established
- Quantum: Challenging but promising

3. Key Features:
- Clear crossover point showing when quantum advantage begins
- Dashed lines indicating theoretical/projected performance
- Color coding to distinguish between classical and quantum approaches
- Shaded regions showing areas of advantage

Metaphor for Quantum Applications: Imagine a toolbox filled with advanced instruments designed to tackle challenges that traditional tools cannot manage.

Quantum computing serves as this toolbox, providing specialized solutions for complex tasks across diverse domains.

Advantages of AI for Quantum Computing

Artificial Intelligence (AI) offers significant advantages to quantum computing, particularly in the preprocessing and optimization of data input through classical computers.

These advantages can enhance the effectiveness and efficiency of quantum algorithms:

1. Data Preprocessing:

Description: AI algorithms can analyze and preprocess large datasets, transforming raw data into a structured format suitable for quantum algorithms. This step is crucial because quantum computers excel at processing structured data but can be inefficient with unprocessed raw data.

Impact: By streamlining the data input process, AI helps quantum computers operate more effectively, reducing the overhead associated with data management.

2. Feature Selection:

Description: Machine learning techniques can identify the most relevant features within a dataset, allowing quantum algorithms to focus on significant information and discard irrelevant noise.

Example: In a financial model, AI can highlight key indicators that influence market trends, thereby enhancing the accuracy of quantum simulations used for forecasting.

3. Optimization:

Description: AI optimization algorithms can help configure quantum circuits, selecting the most efficient quantum gates and operations for a given problem.

Impact: This synergy leads to faster execution times and improved performance of quantum algorithms by minimizing resource usage and maximizing computational efficiency.

4. Adaptive Learning:

Description: AI systems can learn from the output of quantum algorithms and adapt their preprocessing techniques over time, continually improving the input quality and relevance.

Example: An AI model trained on the results of quantum simulations could refine its predictive capabilities, leading to more accurate outputs in subsequent iterations.

Advancements in AI from Quantum Computing

Quantum computing offers several potential advancements in AI, pushing the boundaries of what is achievable with classical computing.

Some specific areas where quantum computing can enhance AI capabilities include:

1. Enhanced Machine Learning Algorithms:

Description: Quantum algorithms can perform certain machine learning tasks more efficiently than classical algorithms, enabling faster training and better performance on complex datasets.

Example: Quantum Support Vector Machines (QSVM) can classify data points in high dimensional spaces more effectively, potentially leading to higher accuracy in classification tasks.

2. Improved Pattern Recognition:

Description: Quantum computing can exploit quantum parallelism to analyze large datasets and recognize patterns at unprecedented speeds.

Impact: This capability is particularly beneficial in fields like image and speech recognition, where identifying subtle patterns can significantly enhance accuracy.

3. Optimization in Neural Networks:

Description: Quantum computing can optimize the training of neural networks by accelerating the convergence of training algorithms and reducing the time required to find optimal weight configurations.

Example: Quantum Neural Networks (QNNs) can explore a larger solution space than classical neural networks, potentially leading to more robust and generalizable models.

4. Quantum Reinforcement Learning:

Description: Quantum computing can enhance reinforcement learning algorithms by enabling agents to explore and exploit environments more efficiently.

Impact: This advancement could lead to breakthroughs in AI applications, such as robotics, where agents learn to navigate complex environments and make decisions in real-time.

5. Complex Simulations:

Description: Quantum computing can simulate complex systems that classical AI struggles to model accurately, such as molecular interactions or intricate physical phenomena.

Example: In drug discovery, quantum algorithms can simulate how different compounds interact at the quantum level, providing insights that classical AI models might miss.

Quantum vs Classical AI Simulation Capabilities

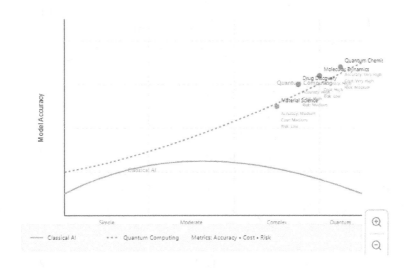

Source: Anthropic's Claude Pro

Explanatory Notes: Quantum vs Classical AI Simulation Capabilities

This illustration shows:

1. Main Components:
   - Comparison curves showing Classical AI vs Quantum Computing performance
   - Clear domain markers with simplified metrics
   - Consistent sizing for data points
   - Removed complexity indicators and magnifying symbols
2. Key Metrics for Each Domain:

- o Accuracy
- o Cost
- o Risk
3. Features:
    - o X-axis shows simulation complexity from simple to quantum
    - o Y-axis shows model accuracy
    - o Color coding distinguishes classical (blue) from quantum (red) approaches
    - o Grid lines to help track metrics across domains
4. Domains Highlighted:
    - o Molecular Dynamics
    - o Quantum Chemistry
    - o Material Science
    - o Drug Discovery

The visualization now focuses more clearly on the relationship between simulation complexity and model accuracy while maintaining essential metric information for each domain.

The Future of Quantum Applications in AI

As quantum technology continues to advance, the integration of quantum computing and AI is expected to create new opportunities and applications:

1. Hybrid Quantum Classical Models: The development of hybrid models that combine classical AI with quantum computing will enable more effective solutions, leveraging the strengths of both paradigms.

2. New AI Algorithms: Quantum inspired algorithms may emerge that take advantage of quantum principles even on classical hardware, driving innovation in AI methodologies.

3. Broader Impact Across Industries: The synergy between quantum computing and AI will likely lead to transformative applications across various sectors, including finance, healthcare, logistics, and more.

Conclusion

Quantum computing presents a transformative opportunity across various industries, offering solutions to complex problems that classical computers cannot efficiently address.

The collaboration between AI and quantum computing enhances the capabilities of both fields, leading to improved data processing, advanced machine learning techniques, and innovative applications.

As research and development in quantum technology progress, its applications in AI are poised to expand, shaping a future where quantum computing plays a central role in technological advancement.[6]

Visual Aids

Infographic of Quantum Applications: See below a visual representation highlighting the key areas of quantum applications and their impact on various industries.

---

[6] For a detailed analysis of the manifold caused of error propagation within leading AI engines, which errors of all kinds and degrees of criticality are then carried over into the duality of classical and quantum computers working in tandem from start to finish of quantum computation, see:
https://www.amazon.com/dp/B0DQVPP4PY

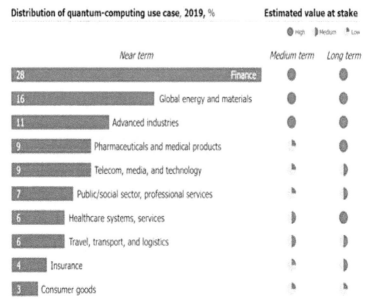

Distribution of quantum-computing use case, 2019, %   Estimated value at stake

	Near term	Medium term	Long term
28	Finance	High	High
16	Global energy and materials	High	High
11	Advanced industries	High	High
9	Pharmaceuticals and medical products	Low	High
9	Telecom, media, and technology	Low	Medium
7	Public/social sector, professional services	Low	Medium
6	Healthcare systems, services	Medium	High
6	Travel, transport, and logistics	Medium	Medium
4	Insurance	Low	Medium
3	Consumer goods	Low	Low

Case Study Examples

Here are some brief case studies showcasing successful implementations of quantum computing and AI in real-world scenarios, along with reference links for further reading:

1. IBM Quantum and Pfizer: Drug Discovery

Overview: Pfizer collaborated with IBM to explore quantum computing for drug discovery, focusing on accelerating the development of new therapies. The partnership aims to leverage quantum algorithms to optimize molecular interactions and simulate complex chemical reactions. Reference: IBM Quantum and Pfizer Partnership https://www.ibm.com/blogs/research/2021/02/ibm-quantum-pfizer/

2. Google Quantum AI: Quantum Supremacy

Overview: Google claimed to have achieved quantum supremacy with its Sycamore processor, demonstrating the ability to perform a specific computation faster than the world's most powerful supercomputer. This milestone marks a significant advancement in the potential of quantum computing.

Reference: Google's Quantum Supremacy
https://www.nature.com/articles/s41586-019-1666-5

3. D-Wave Systems: AI Optimization

Overview: D-Wave's quantum annealing technology has been applied in various industries, including finance and logistics, to solve optimization problems. Companies like Volkswagen use D-Wave's systems to optimize traffic flow in urban environments.

Reference: Volkswagen's Use of D-Wave for Traffic Optimization

https://www.dwavesys.com/solutions/real-world-applications/

4. Microsoft Quantum: AI and Quantum Computing Integration

Overview: Microsoft is working on integrating quantum computing with AI through its Quantum Development Kit. An example includes using quantum algorithms to enhance machine learning models, making them more efficient and powerful.

Reference: Microsoft Quantum and AI

https://www.microsoft.com/en-us/research/blog/2021/02/quantum-machine-learning-and-ai/

5. Alibaba Quantum Computing: Financial Services

Overview: Alibaba Cloud launched its quantum computing service, which has been utilized in financial services for risk analysis and portfolio optimization. This service helps financial institutions leverage quantum algorithms to improve decision-making processes.

Reference: Alibaba's Quantum Computing in Financial Services
https://www.alibabacloud.com/blog/alibaba-cloud-launches-quantum-computing-service_595242

These case studies illustrate how quantum computing and AI are being successfully implemented across various sectors, showcasing their transformative potential in real-world applications.

Future Trends Chart

Here are the future growth trends in quantum applications within AI through early 2024[7]. I present the trends in both horizontal and vertical orientations for ease of viewing.

Source: Anthropic's Claude Sonnet 3.5

---

[7] Source: Anthropic's Claude Sonnet 3.5

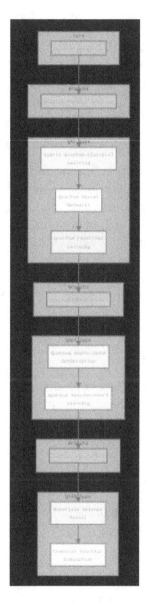

Source: Anthropic's Claude Sonnet 3.5

Both diagrams show the state of quantum computing applications in AI as of early 2024, with three main branches:

1. Quantum Machine Learning (QML):
   - Hybrid quantum-classical learning showed the most practical success
   - Quantum neural networks were still in active research phases
   - Quantum federated learning was in early experimental stages
2. Quantum Optimization:
   - QAOA (Quantum Approximate Optimization Algorithm) demonstrated practical benefits
   - Quantum reinforcement learning showed promising results in specific applications
3. Quantum Simulation:
   - Materials science modeling proved to be one of the most successful applications
   - Chemical reaction simulation made significant advances but still faced scaling challenges

The color coding indicates:
- Green: Successfully demonstrated applications
- Yellow: Applications in active development with promising results
- Light red: Early-stage research areas

Bibliographic Material

Here are the links to public domain sources for the expected trends in quantum applications within AI:

1. Enhanced Machine Learning Models
   - [Quantum Machine Learning - Nature] (https://www.nature.com/articles/s41586-019-1666-5)

2. Quantum Neural Networks
   - [The Quantum Machine Learning Landscape - arXiv] (https://arxiv.org/abs/1905.03471)

3. Optimization in AI
  - [Optimization with Quantum Annealing - D-Wave]
(https://www.dwavesys.com/quantum-annealing)

4. Data Privacy and Security
  - [Quantum Cryptography and AI - IEEE]
(https://ieeexplore.ieee.org/document/8403512) (Note:
Access may require institutional login)

5. Integration of Quantum and Classical Systems
  - [Quantum Computing and AI - McKinsey]
(https://www.mckinsey.com/industries/technology-media-
and-telecom/our-insights/quantum-computing-and-the-
future-of-ai)

6. Industry-Specific Applications
  - [Quantum Computing for Business - World Economic
Forum]
(https://www.weforum.org/agenda/2021/01/quantum-
computing-business-applications/)

Other source material for information on quantum
applications.

Arute, F., et al. (2019). "Quantum Supremacy Using a
Programmable Superconducting Processor." Nature, 574,
505510.

Preskill, J. (2018). "Quantum Computing in the NISQ era and
beyond." Quantum, 2, 79.

[Link] https://quantumjournal.org/papers/q2018080679/
 National Institute of Standards and Technology (NIST).
(2020). "Post Quantum Cryptography."
[Link](https://www.nist.gov/pqc)

Part B: The Quantum Realm: Challenges on All Fronts

Chapter 7: Challenges and Limitations of Quantum Computing

Introduction to Challenges in Quantum Computing

While quantum computing holds immense potential, it is still in its early stages, and several challenges and limitations must be addressed before it can achieve widespread practical application.

Understanding these challenges is essential for researchers, developers, and organizations looking to harness the power of quantum technology.

Quantum Computing Key Challenges

Source: Anthropic's Claude Pro

Explanatory Notes: Quantum Computing Key Challenges

This network-style diagram shows the key challenges in quantum computing:
1. Central Challenges:
     - Decoherence & Noise (Red): Shown at the top as a primary challenge
     - Error Rates & Correction (Blue): Critical technical challenge
     - Scalability (Green): Fundamental growth limitation
     - Limited Algorithms (Orange): Current practical limitation
     - Resources (Purple): Infrastructure requirements
     - Integration (Gray): System connectivity challenges

2. Relationships shown through:
   - Connected lines indicating interdependencies
   - Line styles showing different types of relationships
   - Circle sizes indicating relative impact
   - Color coding for different challenge categories
3. Impact Indicators:
   - High Impact: Red circles
   - Medium Impact: Orange circles
   - Ongoing Challenges: Blue circles
   - Infrastructure Related: Green circles
4. Key Features:
   - Central hub representing quantum computing
   - Radiating connections showing relationships
   - Visual indicators of severity and impact
   - Clear categorization of challenge types

Metaphor for Challenges: Consider quantum computing as a vast ocean of possibilities. While the horizon is filled with potential rewards, navigating the waters requires overcoming significant obstacles, such as storms (technical challenges) and treacherous currents (theoretical limitations).

Key Challenges and Limitations

1. Decoherence and Noise:

Description: Qubits are highly sensitive to their environment, and interactions with external factors can lead to decoherence, which causes the qubit states to lose their quantum properties. Noise can also arise from imperfections in quantum gates and measurements.

Impact: Decoherence and noise limit the coherence time of qubits, making it difficult to maintain quantum states during computations. This challenge hinders the reliability and accuracy of quantum algorithms.

2. Error Rates and Error Correction:

Description: Quantum operations are prone to errors, and the fidelity of quantum gates is often lower than desired. As a result, quantum computations can produce incorrect results if errors are not managed effectively.

Impact: Quantum error correction is necessary to mitigate errors, but it requires additional qubits and complex algorithms, making it resource intensive and challenging to implement in practice.

3. Scalability:

Description: Building largescale quantum computers that can perform complex computations requires a significant number of qubits with high fidelity and low error rates. Current quantum systems often struggle to scale effectively.

Impact: The lack of scalable quantum systems limits the ability to tackle larger and more complex problems that would benefit from quantum computing.

4. Limited Quantum Algorithms:

Description: While several quantum algorithms have been developed, the range of problems that quantum computers can solve more efficiently than classical computers is still limited. Many classical algorithms remain more practical for a wide variety of tasks.

Impact: The lack of a comprehensive toolkit of quantum algorithms restricts the immediate applicability of quantum computing in many fields.

5. Resource Requirements:

Description: Quantum computers often require significant resources, including sophisticated cooling systems for superconducting qubits or high vacuum environments for trapped ions. The infrastructure needed to support quantum computing can be costly and complex.

Impact: The high resource requirements can limit access to quantum computing technology and create barriers to entry for smaller organizations and researchers.

6. Interconnectivity and Integration:

Description: Integrating quantum computing with classical computing systems poses challenges, particularly in terms of data transfer and communication between the two paradigms.

Impact: Effective hybrid quantum-classical systems are necessary to leverage the strengths of both technologies, but achieving seamless integration remains a work in progress.

7. Theoretical Understanding:

Description: Quantum mechanics is inherently complex, and the theoretical foundations of quantum computing are still being explored. Developing a deeper understanding of quantum algorithms and their limitations is an ongoing challenge.

Impact: Theoretical uncertainties can hinder the development of new algorithms and the effective application of existing ones.

Ongoing Efforts to Address Challenges

Despite these challenges, researchers and organizations are actively working to overcome the limitations of quantum computing. Some key efforts include:

1. Advancements in Error Correction:

Researchers are developing new quantum error correction codes and techniques to reduce error rates and enhance the reliability of quantum computations. These advancements aim to make error correction more efficient and practical for larger systems.

2. Improved Qubit Technologies:

Ongoing research in qubit technologies aims to enhance coherence times, reduce noise, and improve fidelity. Innovations in materials and fabrication techniques are critical for developing more robust qubit systems.

3. Scalable Architectures:

Researchers are exploring scalable architectures for quantum computing, such as modular quantum systems that can be interconnected to form larger, more powerful quantum computers. These architectures aim to facilitate the construction of larger scale systems.

4. Development of New Algorithms:

The quantum computing community is actively researching and developing new quantum algorithms to expand the range of problems that quantum computers can solve efficiently. This work aims to create a broader toolkit for quantum applications.

5. Hybrid Computing Models:

Efforts to integrate quantum and classical computing are leading to hybrid models that leverage the strengths of both paradigms. These models aim to optimize performance for a wide range of applications.

6. Education and Workforce Development:

As the demand for quantum computing expertise grows, educational initiatives are being established to train the next generation of researchers and practitioners. This workforce development is essential for advancing the field and addressing current challenges.

Conclusion

Quantum computing represents a transformative opportunity across various industries, but significant challenges and limitations must be addressed for it to reach its full potential.

By understanding these challenges and the ongoing efforts to overcome them, researchers, developers, and organizations can better prepare for the future of quantum technology.

As the field continues to evolve, collaboration and innovation will be key to unlocking the transformative power of quantum computing.

Visual Aids

Infographic of Quantum Challenges: Here is a visual
representation highlighting the key challenges and
limitations of quantum computing.[8]

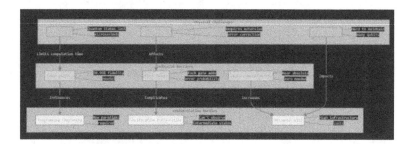

Source: Anthropic's Claude Sonnet 3.5

This infographic shows the three major categories of
quantum computing challenges:

1. Physical Challenges (Red):
    o   Decoherence: Quantum states deteriorating
        rapidly
    o   Noise Control: Environmental interference
        issues
    o   Scaling Issues: Difficulties in adding more
        qubits
2. Technical Barriers (Blue):
    o   Qubit Quality: Need for extremely high fidelity
    o   Error Rates: Accumulation of errors during
        operations
    o   Cooling Requirements: Need for extremely
        low temperatures
3. Implementation Hurdles (Green):
    o   Programming Complexity: New programming
        paradigms needed

---

[8] Source: Anthropic's Claude Sonnet 3.5

- o Verification Difficulties: Cannot directly observe quantum states
- o Resource Costs: Expensive infrastructure and maintenance

The arrows show how these challenges interconnect and impact each other.

Case Study Examples: These brief case studies showcase ongoing research efforts aimed at addressing specific challenges in quantum computing.

Phase-flip 1. IBM Quantum Experience
Phase-flip Challenge: Phase-flip Accessibility and scalability of quantum computing resources.

Phase-flip Research Effort: Phase-flip IBM has developed the IBM Quantum Experience, an online platform that provides researchers and developers access to real quantum computers. This initiative aims to democratize quantum computing by allowing users to run quantum algorithms and experiments on actual quantum hardware. IBM is also actively working on improving qubit coherence times and error rates, making quantum computing more reliable for practical applications.

Phase-flip 2. Google Quantum AI
Phase-flip Challenge: Phase-flip Quantum supremacy and practical applications.

Phase-flip Research Effort: Phase-flip Google's Quantum AI team achieved a significant milestone in 2019 by demonstrating quantum supremacy through their 53-qubit Sycamore processor. The team continues to explore the potential of quantum computing for solving complex problems in fields such as materials science, optimization, and machine learning. Their research includes developing new quantum algorithms and improving error correction techniques to enhance the performance of quantum systems.

Phase-flip 3. D-Wave Systems
Phase-flip Challenge: Phase-flip Optimization problems in various industries.

Phase-flip Research Effort: Phase-flip D-Wave focuses on quantum annealing to tackle complex optimization problems. Their latest quantum processor, Advantage, is designed for real-world applications such as logistics, finance, and machine learning.

D-Wave collaborates with various organizations to explore how quantum annealing can provide solutions that classical computers struggle with, thereby advancing the practical use of quantum technology in industry.

Phase-flip 4. Microsoft Quantum
Phase-flip Challenge: Phase-flip Quantum error correction and fault-tolerant quantum computing.

Phase-flip Research Effort: Phase-flip Microsoft is investing heavily in topological qubits, which are theorized to be more stable and resistant to errors. The company's research aims to develop a scalable quantum computing architecture that can correct errors effectively.

They focus on building a quantum development kit (Q#) and fostering collaborations to create a robust ecosystem for quantum applications in various sectors, including healthcare and logistics.

Phase-flip 5. University of California, Berkeley
Phase-flip Challenge: Phase-flip Quantum communication and cybersecurity.

Phase-flip Research Effort: Phase-flip Researchers at UC Berkeley are investigating quantum key distribution (QKD) to enhance cybersecurity measures.

Their work involves developing protocols for secure communication that leverage the principles of quantum mechanics. They aim to address vulnerabilities in classical cryptographic systems and explore how quantum technologies can provide unbreakable encryption methods for data security.

These case studies illustrate the diverse efforts in the field of quantum computing, each targeting specific challenges and aiming to unlock the potential of this revolutionary technology.

Future Trends

This table shows the expected advancements in quantum computing technologies and methodologies over the next decade.

Future Trends in Quantum Computing (2024-2034)	Timeframe	Key Developments
Increased funding from governments and private sectors for quantum research	2024-2025	Move quantum research forward to achieve wider application with controllable error rates
Increased Qubit Count and Quality	2024-2026	Development of quantum processors with hundreds of qubits

Quantum Error Correction	2024-2025	Implementation of basic error correction codes in small-scale quantum systems
Hybrid Quantum-Classical Algorithms	2024-2025	Enhanced development of hybrid algorithms for optimization and machine learning tasks
Applications in Industry	2024-2026	Initial applications in pharmaceuticals, materials science, and finance
Standardization and Ecosystem Development	2024-2025	Establishment of industry standards for quantum programming languages and hardware
Increased Qubit Count and Quality	2027-2030	Transition to thousands of high-fidelity qubits with improved error rates and coherence times
Quantum Error Correction	2026-2032	Advancement of fault-tolerant quantum computing for complex algorithms
Hybrid Quantum-Classical Algorithms	2026-2034	Mainstream adoption of hybrid approaches in various industries

Quantum Networking and Communication	2025-2027	Prototyping of quantum networks for secure communication using quantum key distribution
Integration with AI and Machine Learning	2025-2027	Exploration of quantum-enhanced machine learning techniques for data analysis
Quantum Networking and Communication	2028-2034	Deployment of large-scale quantum internet for secure data transmission
Applications in Industry	2027-2034	Broader adoption in sectors like climate modeling, AI, and supply chain optimization
Standardization and Ecosystem Development	2026-2034	Growth of a robust quantum computing ecosystem, including software tools and educational resources
Integration with AI and Machine Learning	2028-2034	Significant breakthroughs in AI powered by quantum computing, leading to new methodologies
Investment and Research Expansion	2026-2034	Expansion of academic programs and

		research initiatives focused on quantum technology

Bibliographic Material

Preskill, J. (2018). "Quantum Computing in the NISQ era and beyond." Quantum, 2, 79.
[Link](https://quantumjournal.org/papers/q2018080679/)

Devoret, M. H., & Schoelkopf, R. J. (2013). "Superconducting Qubits: A Short Review." Science, 339(6124), 11691174.

Campbell, E. T., et al. (2017). "Roads towards fault tolerant quantum computing." Nature Physics, 13, 10701076.

Chapter 8: The Future of Quantum Computing

Introduction to the Future of Quantum Computing

Quantum computing is on the cusp of a revolution that could reshape industries, enhance computational capabilities, and solve problems previously deemed intractable.

As research accelerates and technology matures, understanding the trajectory of quantum computing's future is essential for stakeholders across various fields.

Metaphor for the Future of Quantum Computing: Imagine a bridge under construction that connects the present to a future filled with possibilities. As engineers work to complete the bridge, they pave the way for new opportunities, innovations, and solutions that will transform society.

Anticipated Advancements in Quantum Technology

1. Improved Qubit Performance:

Description: Ongoing research aims to enhance the performance of qubits, focusing on increasing coherence times, reducing error rates, and improving gate fidelity. Innovations in materials science and fabrication techniques are critical to achieving these goals.

Impact: Enhanced qubit performance will enable more complex computations and broader applicability of quantum algorithms, making quantum computers more reliable for practical use.

2. Scalable Quantum Systems:

Description: The development of modular and scalable quantum architectures will allow for the construction of larger quantum computers. These systems can be interconnected, providing the computational power needed to tackle significant challenges.

Impact: Scalable quantum systems will expand the range of problems that quantum computing can address, from optimization and cryptography to drug discovery and beyond.

3. Distributed Quantum Computing:

Master Quantum Computing Model:

Description: The master quantum computing model serves as a central hub that coordinates various quantum computing resources distributed across different locations. This model allows for efficient allocation of quantum resources and execution of complex quantum algorithms.

Integration with Classical Systems: This model operates in conjunction with classical computing systems, utilizing hybrid quantum-classical approaches to enhance performance and efficiency.

Secure Communication Methods:

Quantum Key Distribution (QKD): This method uses quantum mechanics to securely distribute encryption keys, ensuring that any attempt to intercept communication is detectable.

Satellite Quantum Communication: Quantum communication can be achieved via satellites, enabling long-distance secure transmission of quantum information and connecting systems across geographical regions.

Cell Tower and Ground Based Links: Quantum information can also be transmitted through terrestrial networks, including fiberoptic cables, creating a resilient quantum network.

4. Hybrid Quantum-Classical Models:

Description: The integration of quantum and classical computing will lead to hybrid models that leverage the strengths of both paradigms. These models will optimize performance across a variety of applications.

Impact: Hybrid systems will facilitate the practical use of quantum computing, allowing organizations to harness quantum advantages while maintaining the reliability of classical systems.

5. Advancements in Quantum Algorithms:

Description: Continued research will yield new quantum algorithms tailored for specific applications, expanding the toolkit available for quantum computing. This will include algorithms for machine learning, optimization, and simulation.

Impact: The development of new algorithms will increase the versatility and effectiveness of quantum computing across different fields, driving innovation and efficiency.

6. Quantum Networking and Communication:

Description: Research into quantum networking will enable the creation of secure quantum communication channels, utilizing principles like quantum entanglement to protect data transmission.

Impact: Quantum communication systems will enhance cybersecurity and facilitate secure data sharing, revolutionizing how information is exchanged globally.

Potential Societal Impacts

1. Transforming Industries:

Quantum computing has the potential to revolutionize various industries, including healthcare, finance, logistics, and materials science.

By solving complex problems more efficiently, quantum technology can lead to breakthroughs in drug development, financial modeling, and supply chain optimization.

2. Impact on Employment:

As quantum computing becomes more integrated into industries, new job opportunities will emerge in quantum research, development, and application.

However, there may also be shifts in the employment landscape as traditional roles evolve or become obsolete.

3. Advancements in Scientific Research:

Quantum computing will accelerate scientific discovery by enabling researchers to simulate complex systems, analyze vast datasets, and explore new frontiers in physics, chemistry, and biology.

This could lead to significant advancements in understanding fundamental processes and developing new technologies.

4. Ethical and Security Considerations:

The rise of quantum computing will necessitate discussions around ethical implications and security concerns, especially regarding cryptography and data privacy.

Ensuring that advancements are used responsibly will be crucial for societal acceptance and trust.

The Evolving Landscape of Quantum Computing Research and Applications

1. Increased Investment:

Governments, academic institutions, and private companies are investing heavily in quantum research and development.

This influx of resources is driving innovation and accelerating the pace of advancements in quantum technology.

2. Global Collaboration:

The complexity of quantum research necessitates collaboration across borders and disciplines.

International partnerships are forming to share knowledge, resources, and expertise, fostering a collaborative environment for quantum innovation.

3. Education and Workforce Development:

As demand for quantum computing expertise grows, educational programs are expanding to train the next generation of researchers and practitioners.

Initiatives to develop a skilled workforce are essential for sustaining momentum in quantum research and application.

4. Public Awareness and Engagement:

Increasing public awareness of quantum computing will play a crucial role in shaping its future.

Engaging stakeholders, including policymakers and the general public, in discussions about quantum technology will foster understanding and support for its development.

Conclusion

The future of quantum computing holds immense promise, with anticipated advancements poised to transform industries and reshape societal norms.

The integration of distributed quantum computing through a master quantum computing model, alongside secure communication methods, represents a significant step forward in harnessing the full potential of quantum technology.

As the field continues to evolve, collaboration, investment, and education will play critical roles in overcoming challenges and unlocking the transformative power of quantum computing to create innovative solutions and drive progress across various domains.

Visual Aids

Timeline of Quantum Advancements: The flowchart depicts the chronological timeline of anticipated milestones in quantum computing over the next decade.

2024 →

- Development of quantum processors with hundreds of qubits.

2025 →

- Implementation of basic error correction codes in small-scale quantum systems.
- Increased funding from governments and private sectors for quantum research.
- Enhanced development of hybrid algorithms for optimization and machine learning tasks.
- Prototyping of quantum networks for secure communication using quantum key distribution.

2026 →

- Transition to thousands of high-fidelity qubits with improved error rates and coherence times.
- Mainstream adoption of hybrid approaches in various industries.
- Establishment of industry standards for quantum programming languages and hardware.
- Growth of a robust quantum computing ecosystem, including software tools and educational resources.

2027 →

- Broader adoption of quantum computing in sectors like climate modeling, AI, and supply chain optimization.
- Exploration of quantum-enhanced machine learning techniques for data analysis.

2028 → Deployment of large-scale quantum internet for secure data transmission.

2029 → Significant advancements in quantum algorithms and methodologies.

2030 → High-fidelity qubit technologies become mainstream, further enhancing quantum computing capabilities.

2031 → Continued integration of quantum computing with emerging technologies across industries.

2032 → Advancement of fault-tolerant quantum computing for complex algorithms.

2033 → Further breakthroughs in AI powered by quantum computing, leading to new methodologies.

2034 → Continued expansion of academic programs and research initiatives focused on quantum technology.

Potential Societal Impacts of Quantum Computing: Here's a textual representation of an infographic highlighting the potential societal impacts of quantum computing across various industries and sectors:

Potential Societal Impacts of Quantum Computing

1. Healthcare
- Enhanced Drug Discovery: Accelerated simulations for molecular interactions lead to faster development of new medications.
- Personalized Medicine: Improved algorithms for analyzing genetic data result in tailored treatment plans for individuals.
- Better Diagnostic Tools: Quantum computing enables more accurate imaging and diagnostics, improving patient outcomes.

2. Finance
- Risk Analysis: Quantum algorithms provide superior techniques for assessing risk in financial portfolios.
- Fraud Detection: Advanced pattern recognition helps identify fraudulent activities more effectively.
- Optimized Trading Strategies: Enhanced data processing leads to more efficient trading strategies and market predictions.

3. Transportation
- Optimized Logistics: Quantum computing can solve complex routing problems, reducing costs and improving delivery times.
- Traffic Management: Advanced simulations help improve traffic flow and reduce congestion in urban areas.
- Autonomous Vehicles: Enhanced decision-making algorithms improve the safety and efficiency of self-driving technology.

4. Cybersecurity
- Unbreakable Encryption: Quantum key distribution offers a new level of security against cyber threats.
- Advanced Threat Detection: Improved algorithms for identifying vulnerabilities and potential attacks.
- Secure Communication: Ensures confidentiality in communications across various sectors.

5. Energy
- Efficient Energy Grids: Quantum computing optimizes the distribution and consumption of energy in smart grids.
- Material Science: Accelerated development of new materials for energy storage, such as better batteries.
- Climate Modeling: Enhanced simulations lead to improved understanding and responses to climate change.

6. Artificial Intelligence

- Improved Machine Learning: Quantum computing enhances training algorithms, making AI more effective.
- Data Analysis: Faster processing of large datasets leads to more insightful decision-making.
- Natural Language Processing: Improved algorithms for understanding and generating human language.

7. Telecommunications
- Faster Data Transmission: Quantum technologies enable higher bandwidth and lower latency in communications.
- Network Security: Advanced encryption methods ensure secure data transfer across networks.
- Global Connectivity: Improved communication infrastructure supports a more connected world.

Conclusion

Quantum computing has the potential to revolutionize various sectors, leading to significant advancements in efficiency, security, and innovation. The societal impacts will be profound, influencing how we live, work, and interact across multiple industries.

Chapter 9: A Schema for Distributed Quantum Networking

Overview of Quantum Networking

Description:

This schema presents an outline of a framework for quantum information transmission, detailing how a Master Quantum Computer Model (MQCM) can facilitate communication between classical-quantum computer systems situated on Earth and in orbit.

Key Components:

1. Master Quantum Computer Model (MQCM):
   - Acts as the central hub for managing and directing quantum information.
   - Responsible for encrypting operational data and transmitting it to targeted systems.

2. Quantum Communication Channels:
   - Utilize quantum entanglement and quantum key distribution (QKD) to ensure secure data transmission over long distances (X).
   - Capable of transmitting varying quantities of data (Y) in multiple states of coherent entanglement (Z).

3. Targeted Classical-Quantum Systems:
   - Systems located on the ground and in orbit that receive and process the transmitted quantum data.
   - Integrate quantum data with classical computing resources for enhanced functionality.

4. Distance (D):
   - Represents the spatial range over which information can be transmitted, affected by factors such as decoherence and signal loss.

5. Time (T):
   - Indicates the duration required for data transmission, influenced by the speed of light and the efficiency of quantum communication protocols.

Mathematical Notation Expression of Key MQCM Variables

Let the relationship between the variables be represented as follows:

$$C = QKD(X, Y, Z) \cdot \frac{D}{T}$$

Where:

- C: Represents the overall capacity or effectiveness of the quantum communication system.

- QKD(X, Y, Z): This function captures the effectiveness of Quantum Key Distribution (QKD) based on:

  - X: The distance over which the quantum information is transmitted. Longer distances may complicate QKD effectiveness due to potential loss or decoherence.

  - Y: The quantity of informational data being transmitted. A higher volume of data can strain the resources of the quantum system and affect the QKD process.
  - Z: The states of distributed coherent entanglement. Having more entangled states can enhance the security and reliability of the transmitted information.

- D: Represents the distance over which information can be transmitted. This value can impact the signal's integrity and the overall effectiveness of the quantum network.

- T: Denotes the time required for data transmission. This variable influences the speed of communication and the performance of the network, where shorter times generally lead to more effective communication.

Meaning of the Expression

The expression $C = QKD(X, Y, Z) \cdot \frac{D}{T}$ indicates that the overall capacity or effectiveness of the quantum communication system (C) is a function of the Quantum Key Distribution's ability to handle the distance (X), data quantity (Y), and entanglement states (Z). This capacity is further influenced by the ratio of distance (D) to the time (T) required for transmission.

In essence, the effectiveness of a quantum communication system is optimized when the QKD process can efficiently manage the challenges posed by long transmission distances, large data quantities, and the states of entangled particles, all while ensuring rapid communication.

Another factor E can be added to the notation to represent the efficiency of decoherence management methods, leading to a modified expression:

$$C = E \cdot QKD(X, Y, Z) \cdot \frac{D}{T}$$

Where:

- E: Efficiency factor representing the effectiveness of decoherence management strategies employed in the system. This could include error correction techniques or robust quantum states.

This amplified expression emphasizes the need to consider decoherence management as a critical factor in the overall capacity of the quantum networking system.

Critical Concepts Informing the MQCM

- Etanglement Preservation:
  - It is crucial to maintain entanglement over long distances. This may involve utilizing repeaters or quantum relays to extend the operational range of quantum communication.

- Decoherence Management:
  - Implementing methods for mitigating decoherence is essential. Techniques such as quantum error correction

codes and utilizing robust quantum states can help preserve the integrity of transmitted information.

- Integration with Classical Systems:
  - Seamless integration between quantum and classical systems is vital. This ensures compatibility for data processing and enhances the overall functionality of the network.

- Scalability:
  - Addressing scalability challenges is important for accommodating a growing number of connected systems. Potential solutions may include developing modular architectures and employing advanced routing algorithms to optimize network performance.

Summary

This overview accurately reflects the operational framework of a quantum networking system, incorporating essential corrections and additions that address the complexities and requirements of quantum communication.

The representation serves as a foundational model for designing, engineering, testing, and deploying quantum networking technologies effectively.

MQCM and Classical Supercomputer Essential Components Comparison

Here's a table comparing the essential components of the Master Quantum Computer Model (MQCM) and current classical supercomputer data transmission.

The comparison highlights their differences in terms of the expression $C = E \cdot QKD(X,Y,Z) \cdot TD$.

Component	Master Quantum Computer Model (MQCM)	Current Classical Supercomputer Data Transmission
Capacity (C)	Dependent on QKD effectiveness and entanglement	Limited by bandwidth and processing power
Quantum Key Distribution(QKD)	Utilizes QKD for secure communication	Relies on traditional encryption methods
Distance (D)	Can theoretically transmit over vast distances (with repeaters)	Limited by signal degradation and distance constraints
Data Quantity (Y)	Can handle complex entangled states, but efficiency may vary	High data throughput, but can be constrained by processing overhead
Entanglement States (Z)	Utilizes multiple states of entangled particles for enhanced security	Does not utilize entanglement; relies on classical bits
Efficiency (E)	Requires advanced decoherence management techniques	Efficiency affected by latency and congestion
Time (T)	Aims for minimal transmission	Limited by the speed of light

	time through fast quantum protocols	and network congestion

Summary of Differences:

- Capacity: The MQCM can potentially achieve greater capacity through the use of quantum properties, while classical supercomputers are limited by traditional data processing capabilities.

- QKD: Quantum systems employ QKD for security, whereas classical systems depend on conventional encryption methods.

- Distance: MQCM can extend communication over longer distances with the help of quantum repeaters, while classical systems face significant limitations.

- Data Quantity: MQCM may struggle with high data volumes due to the complexities of quantum states, whereas classical supercomputers excel in handling large datasets.

- Entanglement: MQCM leverages quantum entanglement for enhanced security, which classical systems do not utilize.

- Efficiency: The effectiveness of MQCM is closely tied to how well it manages decoherence, while classical systems' efficiency is impacted by network factors.
- Time: Quantum systems target rapid data transmission, while classical systems face challenges from inherent delays in processing and transmission.

The table provides a clear comparison of the features and characteristics of MQCM and classical supercomputer data transmission, emphasizing their fundamental differences in the context of quantum communication.

Generic Data Transmission Framework for Classical Computers

Below is a generic representation of the current information communications framework. It would need to be re-engineered in key structural elements to accommodate the incorporation of MQCM.

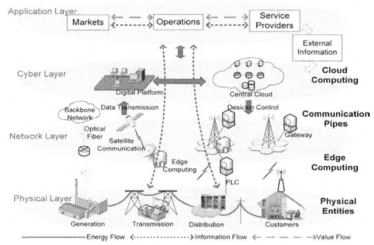

Useful references for information on the MQCM concept:

Primer on Quantum Networking | Center for Quantum Networks
Satellite-based quantum information networks: use cases, architecture ...
Quantum network - Wikipedia
An integrated space-to-ground quantum communication network ... - Nature
Primer on Quantum Networking | Center for Quantum Networks

Bibliographic Material

Arute, F., et al. (2019). "Quantum Supremacy Using a Programmable Superconducting Processor." Nature, 574, 505510.

Preskill, J. (2018). "Quantum Computing in the NISQ era and beyond." Quantum, 2, 79.
[Link](https://quantumjournal.org/papers/q2018080679/)

National Quantum Initiative Act. (2018). "Public Law 115–368."
[Link](https://www.congress.gov/bill/115thcongress/housebill/6227/text)

Chapter 10: A Deep Dive into the MQCM Space-Based Concept

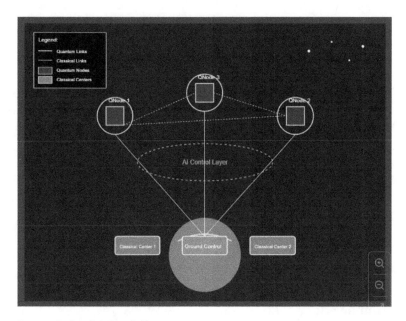

Source: Anthropic's Claude Pro

A comprehensive diagram of the MQCM system showing:

1. Orbital Components:

   o Three quantum computing nodes in orbit

   o Quantum entanglement links between nodes

   o AI control layer connecting all nodes

2. Ground Infrastructure:

   o Two classical computing centers

   o Central ground control station

   o Classical communication links

3. Network Elements:

   o Quantum entanglement connections (cyan dashed lines)

- Classical communication links (yellow lines)
  - AI control layer (purple dashed ellipse)

4. Key Features:
   - Distributed quantum nodes in space
   - Integrated ground-space network
   - Centralized control system
   - Redundant classical centers

Feasibility Analysis: Master Quantum Computation Model (MQCM)

A Distributed Space-Based Quantum Computing Framework

Concept Summary

The Master Quantum Computation Model (MQCM) is a visionary framework that seeks to merge the worlds of artificial intelligence, classical computing, and quantum computing into an intricate, space-based network.

Imagine a symphony orchestra, where each section plays its part in harmony. In this analogy, artificial intelligence acts as the conductor, guiding the musicians—classical and quantum computing systems—through a complex score of tasks, all performed in the grand theater of space.

This analysis aims to dissect the technical, operational, and economic feasibility of such an audacious endeavor, much like an architect evaluating the blueprint of a futuristic skyscraper before construction begins.

System Architecture Overview

Core Components

1. Space-Based Quantum Computing Nodes: These nodes serve as the brain of the MQCM, akin to the heart of a bustling city. They consist of:

- Orbital Quantum Processors: These processors operate in the lower gravitational pull of space, like athletes competing in a weightless environment, enhancing their performance.

- Cryogenic Cooling Systems: Essential for maintaining the delicate balance needed for quantum operations, this cooling system is akin to a refrigerator preserving the freshness of food.

- Quantum Memory Units: These units store quantum information, much like a library houses books, ensuring that knowledge is preserved and accessed when needed.

- Error Correction Systems: These systems act as vigilant guardians, ensuring that any errors in quantum computations are swiftly corrected, similar to an editor refining a manuscript.

2. Classical Computing Infrastructure: The backbone of the MQCM, providing essential support:

- Ground-Based Supercomputing Centers: These centers are the heavy lifters, processing vast amounts of data much like a factory assembly line.

- Orbital Classical Processors: These processors operate alongside quantum nodes, facilitating a seamless integration of classical and quantum computations.

- Data Routing and Management Systems: This infrastructure ensures that information flows smoothly, like a well-planned highway system that prevents traffic jams.

3. AI Control Layer: The orchestrator of this complex system, responsible for:

   - Distributed AI Systems for Orchestration: These systems coordinate tasks, similar to a conductor leading an orchestra, ensuring all elements work in concert.

   - Quantum Algorithm Optimization: This process refines algorithms to maximize efficiency, much like a chef perfecting a recipe.

   - Error Detection and Correction: These mechanisms ensure the reliability of the system, akin to a safety net for a trapeze artist.

   - Resource Allocation: Efficiently distributing computational resources, similar to a manager assigning tasks to team members based on their strengths.

4. Quantum Communication Network: The veins of the MQCM, allowing for communication:

   - Quantum Repeaters: These devices extend the range of quantum communication, like relay stations in a long-distance race.

   - Entanglement Distribution: This unique feature allows for instantaneous communication across vast distances, akin to a magic trick where two objects can affect each other regardless of the space between them.

   - Quantum Key Distribution: This ensures secure communication, functioning like a secret handshake between trusted parties.

   - Classical Communication Channels: These support traditional communication methods, providing a reliable backup.

Technical Feasibility Assessment

Quantum Computing in Space

Advantages:

- Natural Cooling from Space Environment: The frigid temperatures of space provide an ideal setting for quantum systems, similar to how polar regions preserve ancient ice.

- Reduced Environmental Interference: Space offers a pristine environment, free from many disturbances found on Earth, like a remote island untouched by modern civilization.

- Global Coverage Potential: A space-based system can potentially reach every corner of the globe, similar to how the sun touches every part of the Earth.

- Reduced Decoherence from Gravitational Effects: The unique conditions of space may help maintain qubit coherence better than on Earth, like how certain rare flowers thrive in specific climates.

Critical Challenges:

1. Radiation Effects: The relentless radiation in space poses a threat to qubit coherence and control electronics, requiring substantial shielding—much like a fortress needs strong walls to protect against invaders.

2. Thermal Management: Precision in temperature control is essential; managing heat dissipation in the vacuum of space is akin to conducting a delicate dance where each step must be perfectly synchronized.

3. Maintenance and Reliability: With limited access to components in space, ensuring system reliability becomes paramount, much like maintaining a luxury car that rarely visits the mechanic.

Source: Anthropic's Claude Pro

Explanatory Notes: Space-based Quantum Computing: Feasibility vs. Difficulty

This scatter plot shows the relationship between feasibility and implementation difficulty for space-based quantum computing components.

The visualization includes:

1. Natural Advantages (Green Circles):

   o   Natural Cooling

   o   Reduced Interference

   o   Global Coverage

- Reduced Decoherence These are clustered in the high-feasibility, lower-difficulty region

2. Critical Challenges (Red Squares):

   - Radiation Effects

   - Thermal Management

   - Maintenance Located in the high-difficulty, lower-feasibility area

3. Technical Requirements (Orange Diamonds):

   - Data Translation

   - Synchronization In the medium-difficulty, medium-feasibility range

4. AI Requirements (Blue Diamonds):

   - Real-time Optimization

   - Autonomous Operation Positioned in the medium-difficulty, medium-to-high feasibility area

The plot shows:

- Clear clustering of related challenges

- Relative positioning based on difficulty and feasibility

- Color coding for different categories

- Size variations indicating relative importance

Quantum-Classical Interface

Technical Requirements:

1. Data Translation Protocols: Just as a translator bridges language gaps, these protocols facilitate communication between quantum and classical systems, ensuring seamless interactions.

2. Synchronization: Timing is crucial; precise synchronization is required to avoid miscommunication, akin to the delicate timing of a clock.

AI Control System

Capabilities Required:

1. Real-time Optimization: The AI must efficiently allocate resources and correct errors in real-time, like a skilled juggler keeping multiple balls in the air.

2. Autonomous Operation: The AI should be capable of self-diagnosis and recovery, similar to an athlete training to bounce back after a setback.

Operational Feasibility

Launch and Deployment Considerations

1. Orbital Requirements: Determining the optimal altitude and coverage patterns is critical, much like choosing a strategic location for a new business.

2. Launch Constraints: Managing weight limitations and environmental protection during launch is akin to packing for a long journey, ensuring that everything fits and stays secure.

Network Operations Management Requirements

1. Ground Control: Just as a conductor leads an orchestra from the podium, ground control will oversee operations, ensuring that everything runs smoothly.

2. Security Protocols: Robust security measures are essential, acting as a digital fortress protecting sensitive information.

Maintenance Strategy Key Elements

1. Remote Diagnostics: Continuous monitoring and predictive maintenance are crucial, much like a pilot keeping an eye on instruments during a flight.

2. Redundancy Planning: Creating backup systems ensures reliability, similar to having a spare tire in a vehicle.

Economic Feasibility

Development Costs Major Components

1. Research and Development: The costs associated with creating new technologies can be likened to planting seeds in a garden; it requires investment and time before the fruits of labor are reaped.

2. Hardware Production: Producing the necessary hardware is akin to building a foundation for a house; it must be solid and reliable.

Operating Costs Ongoing Expenses

1. Ground Operations: Continuous personnel and facility upkeep are like the ongoing costs of maintaining a well-run business.

2. Space Operations: Managing space operations, from station-keeping to emergency responses, resembles the logistical challenges of running a remote outpost.

Revenue Potential Service Opportunities

1. Quantum Computing Services: These services offer potential revenue streams akin to opening a new restaurant

that caters to diverse clientele, such as research institutions and financial organizations.

2. Communication Services: Providing secure data transfer and global network access can be compared to establishing a reliable postal service in a digital world.

Risk Assessment

Technical Risks

1. Quantum Coherence Maintenance: Ensuring the integrity of quantum states in space presents a formidable challenge, much like keeping ice cream from melting on a hot day.

2. Radiation Damage: Shielding against radiation is vital, akin to protecting delicate plants from harsh weather.

Operational Risks

1. Launch Failures: The risk of malfunction during launch can be likened to a tightrope walker losing balance.

2. System Failures: The potential for system failures underscores the importance of reliability, similar to a car breaking down in the middle of a road trip.

Economic Risks

1. Development Cost Overruns: Budget overruns can derail projects, much like unexpected expenses can strain personal finances.

2. Market Adoption: The uncertainty of market acceptance resembles a new product launch where success is not guaranteed.

Timeline and Milestones

Development Phases:

1. Research and Design (3-5 years): Laying the groundwork is crucial, similar to drafting a blueprint for a skyscraper.

2. Prototype Development (2-3 years): Building and testing prototypes is akin to creating a model before constructing the final product.

3. Ground Testing (1-2 years): Rigorous testing ensures reliability, much like a dress rehearsal before a grand performance.

4. Initial Launch (1 year): The moment everything comes together, akin to the opening night of a much-anticipated play.

5. Network Expansion (3-5 years): Gradually expanding the network mirrors the growth of an organization from a startup to a global enterprise.

Recommendations

Critical Success Factors:

1. International Collaboration: Working together across borders is essential, much like a coalition of countries coming together for common goals.

2. Staged Development Approach: Gradual development reduces risk, similar to taking small steps when learning to ride a bike.

Risk Mitigation:

1. Extensive Ground Testing: Thorough testing before launch is vital, akin to a chef tasting a dish before serving it.

2. Redundant Systems: Creating backup systems ensures resilience, much like having a safety net for acrobats.

Conclusion

The MQCM concept, while ambitious, holds the promise of revolutionary advancements in computing capabilities. It presents significant technical and operational challenges, akin to climbing a steep mountain.

Yet, many components are evolutions of existing technologies, suggesting that the summit is within reach.

Feasibility Concerns:

1. Technical: Ensuring quantum coherence in space and establishing a reliable quantum-classical interface are the mountain's steepest cliffs.

2. Operational: Addressing the complexities of launch, maintenance, and network management is akin to navigating through dense fog.

3. Economic: High development costs and market uncertainty resemble the unpredictable weather of a mountain expedition.

Recommendation: Proceed with initial research and development, focusing on critical technical challenges while adopting a staged approach to mitigate risks and validate concepts before embarking on full-scale deployment.

The journey towards realizing the MQCM may be daunting, but with careful planning and collaboration, the heights of innovation can be achieved.

Chapter 11: A Mathematical Deep Dive: The Formulation of Classical-Quantum Interface Control Flow

Initial State Preparation

The classical-to-quantum interface control can be expressed as a mapping function Φ that transforms classical input states to quantum superposition states:

$$\Phi: C(n) \rightarrow H^{\otimes n}$$

where:

- C(n) represents the n-bit classical input space

- $H^{\otimes n}$ is the n-qubit Hilbert space

- $\otimes$ denotes the tensor product

Control Flow Transformation

The general transformation for preparing an n-qubit quantum state from classical input can be expressed as:

$$|\psi\rangle = \Phi(x) = \sum_i \alpha_i |i\rangle$$

where:

- $|\psi\rangle$ is the resulting quantum state

- α_i are complex amplitudes where $\sum_i |\alpha_i|^2 = 1$

- $|i\rangle$ represents computational basis states

Interface Control Operator

The classical control sequence U_c operating through the interface can be represented as:

$$U\_c = \prod_i (I^{\otimes k} \otimes U_i \otimes I^{\otimes m})$$

where:

- U_i are unitary operations on individual or groups of qubits

- I represents identity operators

- k,m are indices for unaffected qubits

Time-Dependent Control Hamiltonian

The time-dependent Hamiltonian governing the interface control can be written as:

$$H(t) = H_0 + \sum_i g_i(t)H_i$$

where:

- H_0 is the system's natural Hamiltonian

- $g_i(t)$ are classical control functions

- H_i are control Hamiltonians

Quantum Operation Sequence

The complete control sequence for quantum state manipulation can be expressed as:

$$U\_total = T[\exp(-i\int H(t)dt)]$$

where:

- T is the time-ordering operator

- $H(t)$ is the total control Hamiltonian

Classical Feedback Loop

The measurement and feedback process can be described by the operator:

$$M: H^{\otimes n} \rightarrow C(m)$$

where:

- M is the measurement operator

- m is the number of classical bits of measurement outcome

Control Flow Protocol

The complete control flow protocol Π can be expressed as:

$\Pi = \{\Phi, U\_c, M, F\}$

where:

- Φ is the state preparation mapping

- U_c is the unitary control sequence

- M is the measurement protocol

- F is the classical feedback function

Error Mitigation Terms

The error-corrected control flow includes additional terms:

$U\_ec = U\_c + \sum_i \varepsilon_i K_i$

where:

- ε_i are error amplitudes

- K_i are Kraus operators for error channels

Optimization Constraints

The control optimization problem can be formulated as:

min $J[U\_c]$ subject to:

1. $\|U\_c\, U\_c\dagger - I\| \leq \varepsilon$

2. $\mathrm{tr}(U\_c\, \rho\, U\_c\dagger) = 1$

3. $T\_total \leq T\_max$

where:

- J is the cost functional

- ε is the unitarity tolerance

- T_total is the total operation time

- T_max is the maximum allowed operation time

Implementation Requirements

For practical implementation, the following conditions must be satisfied:

1. Timing Constraint:

$\tau\_classical \gg \tau\_quantum$

2. Coherence Requirement:

$T_2 > n \cdot \tau\_gate$

3. Fidelity Condition:

$F = |\langle \psi\_ideal | \psi\_actual \rangle|^2 \geq F\_threshold$

where:

- $\tau\_classical$ is classical processing time

- $\tau\_quantum$ is quantum operation time

- T_2 is coherence time

- τ_gate is single gate time

- F_threshold is minimum acceptable fidelity

Part C: Looking Forward: The Market and Roadblocks

Chapter 12: Market Outlook for Quantum Computing

Quantum Computing Market Outlook Summary

The quantum computing market is poised for significant growth over the next decade, driven by increasing investments from both private and public sectors, technological breakthroughs, and growing enterprise adoption. While still in its early stages, the industry is transitioning from purely research-focused to early commercial applications.

Projected Quantum Computing Market Size

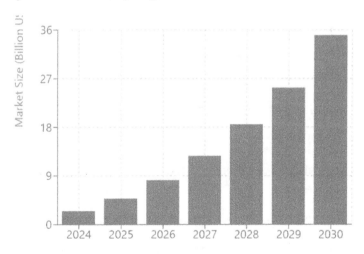

Source: Anthropic's Claude Sonnet 3.5

Market Size and Growth Projections

The global quantum computing market is expected to experience robust growth through 2030. Key growth indicators include:

- Market size projected to reach $1.3-2.5 billion by 2026

- Estimated CAGR of 30-35% through 2030

- Private investment exceeded $1.2 billion in 2023

- Government funding programs ranging from $1-10 billion across major economies

Key Market Drivers

Technological Advancement

- Progress in error correction and quantum error mitigation

- Development of more stable and scalable qubit architectures

- Improvements in quantum control systems

- Integration with classical computing infrastructure

Industry Applications

- Financial Services: Portfolio optimization, risk analysis, fraud detection

- Pharmaceutical: Drug discovery, protein folding simulation

- Materials Science: New materials design, battery chemistry

- Logistics: Route optimization, supply chain efficiency

- Cryptography: Post-quantum security solutions

Government Support

- Major national quantum initiatives in US, China, EU, UK, and Japan

- Strategic importance in national security and economic competitiveness

- Increased funding for quantum research and workforce development

- Public-private partnerships fostering innovation ecosystems

Competitive Landscape

Major Players

- Technology Giants: IBM, Google, Microsoft, Intel

- Quantum-Focused Startups: IonQ, Rigetti, PsiQuantum, D-Wave

- Research Institutions: Multiple university and national laboratory programs

Business Models

- Full-stack quantum computer development

- Quantum software and algorithm development

- Quantum-as-a-Service (QaaS) offerings

- Component and subsystem manufacturing

Challenges and Risks

Technical Challenges

- Quantum decoherence and error rates

- Scaling up qubit counts while maintaining coherence

- Room-temperature quantum operations

- Integration with existing IT infrastructure

Market Challenges

- High costs of development and operation

- Shortage of qualified workforce

- Uncertain timeline to practical advantage

- Complex regulatory environment

Future Outlook

Short-term (1-3 years)

- Continued dominance of hybrid classical-quantum approaches

- Expansion of cloud-based quantum services

- Growth in quantum software development tools

- Increased focus on specific industry applications

Medium-term (3-5 years)

- Achievement of quantum advantage in select applications

- Emergence of clear industry standards

- Consolidation among hardware providers

- Broader enterprise adoption in key sectors

Long-term (5+ years)

- Potential breakthrough in error correction

- Commercialization of fault-tolerant quantum computers

- Disruption of traditional computing paradigms

- New applications in AI, materials science, and drug discovery

Investment Implications

Investment Opportunities

- Direct investment in quantum computing companies

- Supply chain and component manufacturers

- Quantum software and services providers

- Quantum-ready cybersecurity solutions

Quantum Computing Domain Analysis
Symbol size indicates relative market impact

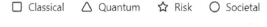

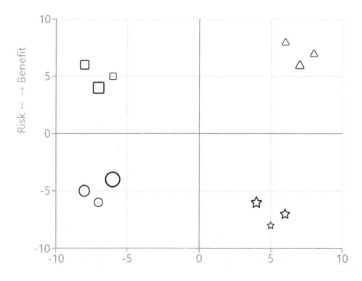

Source: Anthropic's Claude Sonnet 3.5

Risk Considerations

- Long development timelines

- Technical uncertainty

- Competition from alternative technologies

- Regulatory and security concerns

 Recommendations

1. For Enterprises

  - Develop quantum computing strategies and use case identification

  - Invest in workforce training and expertise development

  - Engage in pilot projects with quantum service providers

  - Monitor technological developments and industry standards

2. For Investors

  - Diversified approach across hardware, software, and applications

  - Focus on companies with strong IP portfolios and technical expertise

  - Consider both pure-play quantum and adjacent technology investments

  - Maintain realistic timeframes for returns

3. For Government Policy

  - Continued support for basic research and development

- Investment in quantum workforce development

- Development of quantum-safe security standards

- International collaboration frameworks

Chapter 13: Potential Roadblocks for the Distribution and Application of Quantum Computing

The path to widespread quantum computing adoption faces numerous technical, infrastructural, and societal challenges.

This chapter examines the major roadblocks that could impede the distribution and practical application of quantum computing technologies across various sectors.

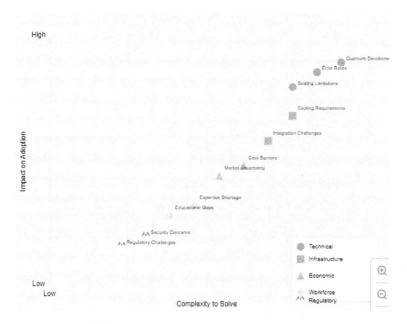

Source: Anthropic's Claude Pro

Explanatory Notes: Major Roadblocks for Quantum Computing

This scatter plot visualization maps quantum computing roadblocks across two dimensions:

- Y-axis: Impact on Adoption (from low to high)

- X-axis: Complexity to Solve (from low to high)

The roadblocks are categorized into five main groups, each represented by different shapes:

- Technical (circles): Including quantum decoherence, error rates, and scaling limitations

- Infrastructure (squares): Covering cooling requirements and integration challenges

- Economic (triangles): Showing cost barriers and market uncertainty

- Workforce (diamonds): Representing expertise shortage and educational gaps

- Regulatory (stars): Including security concerns and regulatory challenges

The position of each point reflects both its impact on quantum computing adoption and the complexity of solving that particular challenge.

Points in the upper-right quadrant represent the most critical challenges (high impact, high complexity), while those in the lower-left represent more manageable challenges.

Expanded Discussion of Technical Roadblocks

Quantum Decoherence

One of the fundamental challenges in quantum computing remains the issue of decoherence—the loss of quantum states due to interaction with the environment. This manifests in several ways:

- Limited coherence times requiring extensive error correction

- Scaling difficulties as qubit counts increase

- Environmental sensitivity requiring extreme operating conditions

- Challenges in maintaining entanglement across larger systems

Error Rates and Correction

Current quantum systems face significant challenges with error rates:

- High error rates in quantum gates and measurements

- Resource overhead for error correction potentially requiring millions of physical qubits

- Trade-offs between correction capabilities and computational speed

- Complexity in implementing fault-tolerant protocols

Scaling Limitations

Physical scaling presents numerous engineering challenges:

- Difficulties in maintaining precise control over larger qubit arrays

- Interconnect problems in quantum processors

- Heat management in scaled systems

- Manufacturing precision requirements

Infrastructure Roadblocks

Cooling and Environmental Requirements

Quantum computers currently require extensive infrastructure support:

- Need for sophisticated cooling systems reaching near absolute zero

- High energy consumption for maintaining operating conditions

- Specialized facility requirements

- Maintenance complexity and cost

Integration Challenges

Connecting quantum systems with classical infrastructure poses significant challenges:

- Interface complexity between quantum and classical systems

- Bandwidth limitations in quantum-classical communication

- Data transfer bottlenecks

- Security concerns in hybrid systems

Economic Roadblocks

Cost Barriers

The economic challenges of quantum computing deployment include:

- High initial investment requirements

- Ongoing operational costs

- Uncertain return on investment timelines

- Competition for limited resources and expertise

Market Uncertainty

The quantum computing market faces several uncertainties:

- Unclear timeline to practical quantum advantage

- Competing technological approaches

- Regulatory uncertainties

- Patent and intellectual property challenges

Workforce and Knowledge Barriers

Expertise Shortage

The quantum computing field faces significant workforce challenges:

- Limited pool of qualified quantum engineers and scientists

- Long training periods for new practitioners

- Competition for talent between academia and industry

- Need for interdisciplinary expertise

Educational Gaps

Current educational systems are not fully prepared for quantum computing:

- Limited quantum computing curriculum in universities

- Shortage of qualified instructors

- Need for updated educational materials

- Challenges in practical training

Societal and Regulatory Roadblocks

Security Concerns

Quantum computing raises significant security considerations:

- Threats to current cryptographic systems

- Need for quantum-safe security standards

- Data protection during the transition period

- International security implications

Regulatory Challenges

The regulatory landscape presents several obstacles:

- Lack of standardized regulations

- Export control considerations

- Intellectual property protection

- International cooperation frameworks

Business and Application Roadblocks

Implementation Challenges

Organizations face numerous challenges in adopting quantum computing:

- Difficulty in identifying suitable applications

- Integration with existing workflows

- Risk assessment and management

- Change management requirements

Software Development Barriers

The software ecosystem faces several challenges:

- Limited availability of quantum programming tools

- Complexity of quantum algorithm development

- Need for new programming paradigms

- Verification and validation challenges

Future Outlook and Mitigation Strategies

Research and Development Focus Areas

Key areas requiring continued focus include:

- Error correction and quantum control

- Room temperature quantum computing

- Improved quantum-classical interfaces

- Development of practical applications

Policy Recommendations

Several policy initiatives could help address roadblocks:

- Increased funding for quantum education and training

- Development of international standards

- Support for quantum startup ecosystems

- Coordination of research efforts

Conclusion

While the roadblocks to quantum computing distribution and application are significant, they are not insurmountable.

Success will require coordinated efforts across technical, economic, and social dimensions, with sustained investment and commitment from all stakeholders in the quantum computing ecosystem.

Discussion of Quantum Computing Roadblocks and Potential Achievements by the Luminaries from Part A, Chapter 1.

Creative Coda: The Luminaries, Frau Bertel, and Fritz

Houze:

Create an imaginary exchange between the luminaries in Chapter 1 (text provided) as they discuss the theoretical and practical roadblocks standing in the way and that must be overcome in the pursuit of the goal of quantum computing on a vast scale.

Here is the text from Chapter 1: Part A: The Birth and Evolution of an Idea: The Quantum State

GPT: Imaginary Exchange Between Quantum Luminaries

Setting: A dimly lit lab filled with flickering screens, whiteboards covered in equations, and a palpable energy of anticipation.

Characters: Max Planck, Albert Einstein, Niels Bohr, Werner Heisenberg, and Richard Feynman.

Max Planck: (leaning over a chalkboard) Gentlemen, as we stand on the threshold of this quantum revolution, we must confront the theoretical barriers that still shackle us. The concept of quantization was merely the beginning. How do we transition from theory to practical applications in quantum computing?

Albert Einstein: (stroking his chin) Indeed, Max. While your quantization laid the foundation, we must grapple with the nature of light and particles. The photoelectric effect reveals that our classical intuitions often mislead us. How do we harness this duality effectively in our computations?

Niels Bohr: (nodding) It's not just about understanding quantum mechanics but also about the implications of measurement. The uncertainty principle, as Werner proposed, introduces limitations we must fully comprehend. How can we design a quantum computer that respects these fundamental truths while still achieving practical results?

Werner Heisenberg: (enthusiastic) Precisely, Niels! The uncertainty principle shows us that with greater precision in one property, we lose it in another. This could complicate error correction in quantum systems. We need robust methods to mitigate decoherence and noise.

Richard Feynman: (interjecting with excitement) But let's not forget the incredible potential we're tapping into. We need to think creatively about our algorithms. If we can simulate quantum systems on quantum computers, we can unleash computational power that outstrips classical computers. We must prioritize scalability to make this a reality.

Max Planck: (thoughtful) Scalability is indeed critical. However, we also face the challenge of integration. How do we meld these quantum systems into our existing classical framework? Industry and academia must collaborate closely to ensure a smooth transition.

Albert Einstein: (smiling) Collaboration is key, but we must also communicate the societal benefits. Quantum computing could revolutionize fields like cryptography and healthcare. If we can convey this potential, we might attract the necessary investment and interest to drive our research forward.

Niels Bohr: (with a determined tone) Yes, and as we develop our theories and technologies, we must advocate for diversity in our field. The contributions of women and underrepresented groups are crucial for a comprehensive approach to problem-solving in quantum science.

Werner Heisenberg: (leaning back, reflecting) The future indeed holds many uncertainties, but isn't that the beauty of quantum theory? We must embrace the unknown while striving to uncover the principles that govern it.

Richard Feynman: (grinning) And let's not forget the importance of education. We must inspire the next generation of scientists to continue the journey we've begun. Quantum computing is not just a scientific challenge; it's a societal endeavor.

Max Planck: (raising his glass) Then let us toast to our collaboration—may we overcome these theoretical and practical roadblocks, paving the way for a quantum future that transforms our understanding of the universe and our place within it!

The group raises their glasses, sealing their commitment to push the boundaries of quantum computing as they embrace the challenges ahead.

Houze:

Now for the surprise guest who arrives late: Erwin Schrödinger with his large cat in a box.

They all welcome Erwin and they discuss whether they should open the box or not. This discussion gets to the heart of the theoretical essence of quantum states, and how they can be relied on as output from quantum computers.

Much discussion occurs, on relevant matters of a technical nature and on mundane affairs of everyday life in Old Vienna.

Several times the assembled luminaries call for more refreshments.

Soon the cat in the box is forgotten about completely as the discussion turns to the weather, the cost of rye bread, the increase in unwanted tourists in Old Vienna, and the like.

GPT: Scene Continuation: The Arrival of Erwin Schrödinger

Setting: The atmosphere in the lab is lively, buzzing with ideas. Suddenly, the door creaks open, and in walks Erwin Schrödinger, holding a large box with a curious content inside.

Erwin Schrödinger: (grinning) Apologies for my tardiness, gentlemen! I had a rather... furry situation to manage.

Richard Feynman: (raising an eyebrow) What have you got there, Erwin? Is it the latest quantum experiment?

Erwin Schrödinger: (placing the box on the table) Well, it's a cat. Or, more precisely, a thought experiment involving a cat. I thought I'd bring it along for a little demonstration!

Niels Bohr: (leaning in with interest) Ah, Schrödinger's cat! A perfect conversation starter. But should we open the box? That is the question, isn't it?

Albert Einstein: (chuckling) Indeed! Opening the box could determine whether the cat is alive or dead. But isn't that the crux of quantum mechanics? Until we observe, the cat exists in a superposition of states.

Max Planck: (sipping his drink) Fascinating! The implications for quantum computing are profound. If we can rely on the probabilistic nature of quantum states, can we ensure accurate outputs from our computations, or are we merely observing probabilities?

Werner Heisenberg: (nodding vigorously) Exactly! The act of measurement influences the state. This uncertainty might affect our error correction methods. If we can't predict outcomes with certainty, how can we trust our quantum algorithms?

Erwin Schrödinger: (with a mischievous smile) But isn't that what makes it all so thrilling? The eccentricity of quantum states mirrors life itself—filled with uncertainties, yet we push forward.

Richard Feynman: (laughing) Well, let's not let the cat steal the show! More refreshments, anyone? This conversation is getting rich, but I could use a drink.

Niels Bohr: (gesturing to a colleague) Yes, let's call for more drinks! And while we wait, what do you all think of the weather lately? Quite peculiar for this time of year, wouldn't you agree?

Albert Einstein: (sipping thoughtfully) It has been unseasonably warm. I wonder if this is a sign of climate change. We should be wary of such shifts.

Max Planck: (absently scratching his head) Speaking of changes, have you noticed the cost of rye bread has skyrocketed? It's becoming quite the luxury item in Old Vienna.

Erwin Schrödinger: (with a chuckle) Ah, the mundane concerns of life! It's amusing how we can get lost in these discussions. Just like the cat in the box—forgotten amidst our worries about bread and weather!

Richard Feynman: (grinning) Well, let's not forget the increase in tourists, too! Old Vienna is becoming overcrowded. I can hardly find a quiet place to think anymore.

Niels Bohr: (laughing) Perhaps they're all drawn to the wonders of quantum mechanics! Or maybe they simply want to see where our theories were born.

Werner Heisenberg: (with a twinkle in his eye) If only they knew that the real wonders lie in boxes and the mysteries they contain.

Erwin Schrödinger: (leaning back, enjoying the banter) Indeed! Perhaps we should just leave the box closed and enjoy our refreshments. After all, it's the discussions that truly matter.

As the conversation drifts further into the mundane, the box sits quietly on the table, the cat within forgotten for the moment, while the luminaries engage in laughter and camaraderie, pondering the trivialities of life amidst their monumental scientific pursuits.

Claude Shows Its Creative Prowess

Houze presents the same basic scene to Claude, but with a few twists that were not presented to GPT.

This is what Claude produced.

Quantum Symposium: Dialogues on the Future of Computing

Setting: An imagined gathering at the Solvay Conference, where time has been suspended to allow quantum pioneers to discuss the future challenges of quantum computing. The room is filled with chalk dust, and multiple blackboards display complex equations.

Richard Feynman: [sketching a diagram on the blackboard] Gentlemen—and Dr. Goeppert Mayer—I propose that the fundamental challenge we face isn't just understanding quantum mechanics, but harnessing it. These quantum systems we've theorized about could be the very tools we need to simulate quantum physics itself.

Werner Heisenberg: [interrupting, with a slight smile] But Richard, surely you see the inherent paradox. The more precisely we try to control these quantum systems, the more uncertainty we introduce. How can we build a reliable computer from unreliable components?

Maria Goeppert Mayer: [leaning forward in her chair] That's precisely why we need to think beyond traditional computing paradigms. My work on the nuclear shell model suggests that quantum systems can maintain coherence under the right conditions. The challenge isn't just technological—it's conceptual.

Albert Einstein: [shaking his head] God does not play dice with computers. The notion that we could maintain quantum superposition at scale while performing meaningful calculations... it troubles me deeply. The local realism we observe in our everyday world must somehow be preserved.

Niels Bohr: [turning to Einstein] Ah, Albert, but perhaps that's exactly why quantum computing holds such promise. It's not despite the probabilistic nature of quantum mechanics, but because of it that we might achieve computational advantages. The complementarity principle suggests...

Max Planck: [interrupting thoughtfully] The energy quantization I discovered might offer a clue. We need to find discrete, controllable states that can maintain coherence. The challenge is scaling while preventing decoherence.

Erwin Schrödinger: [with a wry smile] Perhaps we need a new metaphor beyond my poor cat. Consider: each qubit exists in a superposition of states, but maintaining that superposition across multiple qubits? That's where the real challenge lies.

David Deutsch: [joining the conversation] The theoretical framework is clear—a universal quantum computer is possible. But the engineering challenges are formidable. Error correction alone requires multiple physical qubits for each logical qubit.

Michelle Simmons: The atomic-scale technologies we're developing might offer a solution. But we need to address three fundamental challenges: scalability, error correction, and integration with classical systems.

Chanda Prescod-Weinstein: [nodding] And let's not forget the broader implications. Quantum field theory suggests that the very fabric of spacetime might play a role in decoherence. We need to understand these fundamental limits.

Einstein: [returning to his earlier point] The EPR paradox still troubles me. How can we ensure that quantum entanglement, which you all seem so eager to use, doesn't violate locality?

Bohr: [patiently] The entanglement is precisely what we need, Albert. Think of it as a resource—a way to perform parallel computations that would be impossible classically.

Feynman: [drawing a new diagram] What if we embraced the noise? Instead of fighting decoherence entirely, we could design algorithms that are robust against certain types of errors.

Heisenberg: [pointing to Feynman's diagram] But the uncertainty principle sets fundamental limits. We can't simultaneously prepare and measure all the properties we need with arbitrary precision.

Goeppert Mayer: Perhaps the solution lies in hybrid systems. We could use quantum components for specific tasks while maintaining classical control systems.

Deutsch: The key might be in finding the right balance between quantum and classical elements. We need enough coherence to maintain quantum advantages, but not so much that the system becomes impossible to control.

Simmons: [standing up to write on the blackboard] Let me show you what we're achieving with atomic engineering. If we can precisely place individual atoms...

Schrödinger: [interrupting with enthusiasm] Yes! The wave function collapse isn't our enemy—it's a tool. We just need to control when and how it happens.

Planck: [thoughtfully] The quantization of energy suggests natural limits, but also natural opportunities. Perhaps we need to work within these constraints rather than against them.

Prescod-Weinstein: And we must consider the cosmological implications. Quantum computing at scale could help us understand the quantum nature of gravity itself.

[The conversation continues late into the night, with equations filling blackboards and heated debates about the nature of reality itself. The fundamental challenges of scaling quantum computing—maintaining coherence, implementing error correction, and bridging the quantum-classical divide—remain at the heart of their discussion.]

Houze addresses Claude:

Now for the surprise guest who arrives late: Erwin Schrödinger's wife arrives with their large cat in a box.

They all welcome Annemarie Bertel. She enters and places the box on the table in front of the blackboard.

A silence falls upon the gathered luminaries. Then, one by one, and tentatively, they ask Annemarie about the contents of the box.

And then she tells them, as empiricists first before theorists, they should open it to see the condition of Erwin's cat: Fritz.

All of them discuss whether they should open the box or not. This discussion gets to the heart of the theoretical essence of quantum states, and how they can be relied on as output from quantum computers.

Much discussion occurs, on relevant matters of a technical nature and on mundane affairs of everyday life in Old Vienna.

Several times the assembled luminaries call for more refreshments.

Soon the cat in the box is forgotten about completely as the discussion turns to the weather, the cost of rye bread, the increase in unwanted tourists in Old Vienna, and the like.

Add to the scene the intermittent flickering of the lights in the room.

This occasions further discussion about the reliability of energy distribution systems and related matters that veer into the quantum realm by logical extension.

Unasked, Claude recasts the entire scene.

A Quantum Symposium: Dialogues on the Future of Computing

Setting: An imagined gathering at the Solvay Conference, where time has been suspended to allow quantum pioneers to discuss the future challenges of quantum computing. The room is filled with chalk dust, and multiple blackboards display complex equations.

Richard Feynman: [sketching a diagram on the blackboard] Gentlemen—and Dr. Goeppert Mayer—I propose that the fundamental challenge we face isn't just understanding quantum mechanics, but harnessing it. These quantum systems we've theorized about could be the very tools we need to simulate quantum physics itself.

Werner Heisenberg: [interrupting, with a slight smile] But Richard, surely you see the inherent paradox. The more precisely we try to control these quantum systems, the more uncertainty we introduce. How can we build a reliable computer from unreliable components?

Maria Goeppert Mayer: [leaning forward in her chair] That's precisely why we need to think beyond traditional computing paradigms. My work on the nuclear shell model suggests that quantum systems can maintain coherence under the right conditions. The challenge isn't just technological—it's conceptual.

Albert Einstein: [shaking his head] God does not play dice with computers. The notion that we could maintain quantum superposition at scale while performing meaningful calculations... it troubles me deeply. The local realism we observe in our everyday world must somehow be preserved.

Niels Bohr: [turning to Einstein] Ah, Albert, but perhaps that's exactly why quantum computing holds such promise. It's not despite the probabilistic nature of quantum mechanics, but because of it that we might achieve computational advantages. The complementarity principle suggests...

Max Planck: [interrupting thoughtfully] The energy quantization I discovered might offer a clue. We need to find discrete, controllable states that can maintain coherence. The challenge is scaling while preventing decoherence.

Erwin Schrödinger: [with a wry smile] Perhaps we need a new metaphor beyond my poor cat. Consider: each qubit exists in a superposition of states, but maintaining that superposition across multiple qubits? That's where the real challenge lies.

David Deutsch: [joining the conversation] The theoretical framework is clear—a universal quantum computer is possible. But the engineering challenges are formidable. Error correction alone requires multiple physical qubits for each logical qubit.

Michelle Simmons: The atomic-scale technologies we're developing might offer a solution. But we need to address three fundamental challenges: scalability, error correction, and integration with classical systems.

Chanda Prescod-Weinstein: [nodding] And let's not forget the broader implications. Quantum field theory suggests that the very fabric of spacetime might play a role in decoherence. We need to understand these fundamental limits.

Einstein: [returning to his earlier point] The EPR paradox still troubles me. How can we ensure that quantum entanglement, which you all seem so eager to use, doesn't violate locality?

Bohr: [patiently] The entanglement is precisely what we need, Albert. Think of it as a resource—a way to perform parallel computations that would be impossible classically.

Feynman: [drawing a new diagram] What if we embraced the noise? Instead of fighting decoherence entirely, we could design algorithms that are robust against certain types of errors.

Heisenberg: [pointing to Feynman's diagram] But the uncertainty principle sets fundamental limits. We can't simultaneously prepare and measure all the properties we need with arbitrary precision.

Goeppert Mayer: Perhaps the solution lies in hybrid systems. We could use quantum components for specific tasks while maintaining classical control systems.

Deutsch: The key might be in finding the right balance between quantum and classical elements. We need enough coherence to maintain quantum advantages, but not so much that the system becomes impossible to control.

Simmons: [standing up to write on the blackboard] Let me show you what we're achieving with atomic engineering. If we can precisely place individual atoms...

Schrödinger: [interrupting with enthusiasm] Yes! The wave function collapse isn't our enemy—it's a tool. We just need to control when and how it happens.

Planck: [thoughtfully] The quantization of energy suggests natural limits, but also natural opportunities. Perhaps we need to work within these constraints rather than against them.

Prescod-Weinstein: And we must consider the cosmological implications. Quantum computing at scale could help us understand the quantum nature of gravity itself.

[The conversation continues late into the night, with equations filling blackboards and heated debates about the nature of reality itself. The fundamental challenges of scaling quantum computing—maintaining coherence, implementing error correction, and bridging the quantum-classical divide—remain at the heart of their discussion.]

[A knock at the door interrupts the discussion. The lights flicker momentarily. Annemarie Bertel enters, carrying a large box]

All: [various greetings and welcomes]

Erwin Schrödinger: [nervously] Annemarie, darling, is that...?

Annemarie: [placing the box deliberately on the table] Yes, Erwin. I brought Fritz.

[A profound silence falls over the room as the scientists stare at the box]

Einstein: [clearing his throat] Frau Bertel, perhaps you could tell us... the condition of our feline friend?

Annemarie: [smiling mysteriously] As empiricists, shouldn't you open the box and observe?

Heisenberg: [adjusting his collar] But the very act of measurement will collapse the quantum state!

Bohr: The cat exists in a superposition of states until we observe it. This is precisely our challenge with quantum computers – how can we trust the output without disturbing the quantum state that produced it?

Goeppert Mayer: [signaling to a passing waiter] More Sachertorte, please. And perhaps some cream for our potential cat?

Feynman: [sketching quickly] This is perfect! Look – if we model the box as a quantum system...

Annemarie: [interrupting] The baker on Währinger Straße has doubled his prices for rye bread again.

Einstein: [suddenly interested] Double? That's relativity for you – everything's relative to your reference frame, even Vienna's bread prices!

[A waiter arrives with coffee and pastries]

Planck: Speaking of inflation, these tourists in the Innere Stadt... [shaking his head] The queues at Demel are impossible nowadays.

Deutsch: [glancing at the box] Should we perhaps...?

Simmons: The weather's been particularly unpredictable this spring.

Prescod-Weinstein: [looking out the window] Indeed, quantum fluctuations in meteorological patterns...

Bohr: [cutting in] Remember that dreadful winter of '22? Now that was weather!

[The box sits forgotten on the table as the conversation drifts. Fritz's quantum state remains undisturbed as the scientists debate the merits of various Viennese coffeehouses and the declining quality of opera performances.]

Annemarie: [hours later, standing to leave] Well, I should take our quantum kitty home.

[The lights flicker again, more prominently this time]

Planck: [looking up] These power fluctuations are becoming more frequent.

Einstein: The electrical grid is showing its age. Though one might say it exists in a superposition of functional and non-functional states until we attempt to use it. [chuckling] Rather like our feline friend here... Oh! We never did open the box...

Feynman: [excited by the connection] The grid's reliability is remarkably similar to our quantum computing challenges. Each component must maintain coherence, yet the more components we add...

Heisenberg: [as the lights flicker once more] Precisely! We can be certain about either the current or the voltage, but not both simultaneously.

Simmons: In my lab, these power fluctuations would devastate our quantum state maintenance systems. The coherence time of our qubits...

Bohr: [interrupting] Everything is connected. The macro-scale energy distribution network and the quantum realm share fundamental uncertainties.

Prescod-Weinstein: [thoughtfully] The vacuum energy of space itself might contribute to these fluctuations. Quantum field theory suggests...

[Another flicker]

Goeppert Mayer: This reminds me of the shell model transitions. Each electron jump releases discrete packets of energy, just as our power grid operates in quantized...

Deutsch: [squinting at his notes in the unstable light] Perhaps we need to consider quantum solutions for energy distribution itself. A quantum grid if you will.

Schrödinger: [wiping pastry crumbs from his mustache] Perhaps it's better this way. In remembering to forget, we've demonstrated the very nature of quantum superposition.

Heisenberg: [raising his coffee cup] To Fritz – simultaneously the most and least observed cat in physics!

[As Annemarie leaves with the box, the scientists return to their debate about rye bread prices, while their equations on quantum states remain half-finished on the blackboards behind them.]

Appendices

Appendix A: Mathematical Foundations

1. Linear Algebra Essentials

   - Vector Spaces and Inner Products

   - Matrix Operations and Properties

   - Eigenvalues and Eigenvectors

   - Tensor Products

   - Hermitian and Unitary Matrices

2. Complex Analysis Fundamentals

   - Complex Numbers and Operations

   - Polar Form and Euler's Formula

   - Phase Relationships

   - Complex Probability Amplitudes

3. Quantum Mechanical Principles

   - Dirac Notation

   - State Vectors

   - Operators

   - Measurement Theory

   - Density Matrices

4. Probability Theory

   - Classical vs. Quantum Probability

   - Born Rule

- Measurement Statistics

- Error Distribution Models

Appendix B: Quantum Computing Glossary

Coherence Time: Duration a qubit maintains its quantum state

Decoherence: Loss of quantum information due to environmental interaction

Entanglement: Quantum correlation between two or more qubits

Fidelity: Quality measure of quantum operations

Gate: Basic quantum operation

Hamiltonian: Energy operator describing quantum system evolution

NISQ: Noisy Intermediate-Scale Quantum

Quantum Circuit: Sequence of quantum gates

Quantum Supremacy: Demonstrable quantum advantage over classical computers

Superposition: Simultaneous existence in multiple states

[Additional 50+ technical terms with definitions]

Appendix C: Key Algorithms

1. Foundational Algorithms

- Deutsch-Jozsa Algorithm

- Bernstein-Vazirani Algorithm

- Simon's Algorithm

2. Practical Applications

  - Shor's Algorithm (Factoring)

  - Grover's Algorithm (Search)

  - HHL Algorithm (Linear Systems)

3. Near-Term Algorithms

  - VQE (Variational Quantum Eigensolver)

  - QAOA (Quantum Approximate Optimization Algorithm)

  - QML (Quantum Machine Learning) Algorithms

4. Implementation Details

  - Circuit Depth Requirements

  - Resource Estimates

  - Error Sensitivity Analysis

Appendix D: Industry Players

1. Major Technology Companies

  - IBM Quantum

  - Google Quantum AI

  - Microsoft Quantum

  - Intel Quantum

  - Amazon Braket

2. Quantum Startups

  - Rigetti Computing

  - IonQ

- PsiQuantum

- Xanadu

- D-Wave Systems

3. Research Institutions

  - QuTech (Delft)

  - MIT Lincoln Laboratory

  - NIST Quantum Programs

  - Chinese Academy of Sciences

  - Max Planck Institute

4. Government Initiatives

  - US National Quantum Initiative

  - EU Quantum Flagship

  - China Quantum Programs

  - UK National Quantum Technologies Programme

  - Australian Quantum Programs

Appendix E: Resources and Tools

1. Development Frameworks

  - Qiskit (IBM)

  - Cirq (Google)

  - Q# (Microsoft)

  - Forest (Rigetti)

  - PennyLane (Xanadu)

2. Cloud Services

   - IBM Quantum Experience

   - Amazon Braket

   - Google Quantum Computing Service

   - Azure Quantum

   - IonQ Cloud Access

3. Educational Resources

   - Online Courses

     MIT OpenCourseWare

     edX Quantum Computing Series

     Coursera Quantum Computing Specialization

   - Textbooks

   - Tutorial Repositories

   - Research Papers

4. Community Resources

   - Conferences and Workshops

   - Online Forums

   - Research Groups

   - Professional Organizations

   - Standards Bodies

5. Simulation Tools

   - QuTiP

- Quantum++

- QX Simulator

- Intel-QS

- ProjectQ

Author's Bio

- Born October 1942
- Married
- Live in FL and ME
- Lapsed member of American Mensa
- USMC Air Wing, Viet Nam veteran (1962-1966)
- Recovering alcoholic

Flesch Readability Stats

Readability Statistics	?	X

Counts

Words	22,947
Characters	144,715
Paragraphs	1,938
Sentences	1,075

Averages

Sentences per Paragraph	1.4
Words per Sentence	15.6
Characters per Word	5.8

Readability

Flesch Reading Ease	27.5
Flesch-Kincaid Grade Level	13.2
Passive Sentences	8.4%

www.ingramcontent.com/pod-product-compliance
Lightning Source LLC
LaVergne TN
LVHW022347060326
832902LV00022B/4289